Monty Python's Flying Circus

TV Milestones

Series Editors

Barry Keith Grant
Brock University

Jeanette Sloniowski
Brock University

TV Milestones is part of the Contemporary Approaches to Film and Television Series

A complete listing of the books in this series can be found online at *http://wsupress.wayne.edu*

General Editor

Barry Keith Grant
Brock University

Advisory Editors

Patricia B. Erens
Dominican University

Robert J. Burgoyne
Wayne State University

Lucy Fischer
University of Pittsburgh

Tom Gunning
University of Chicago

Peter Lehman
Arizona State University

Anna McCarthy
New York University

Caren J. Deming
University of Arizona

Peter X. Feng
University of Delaware

Monty Python's FLYING CIRCUS

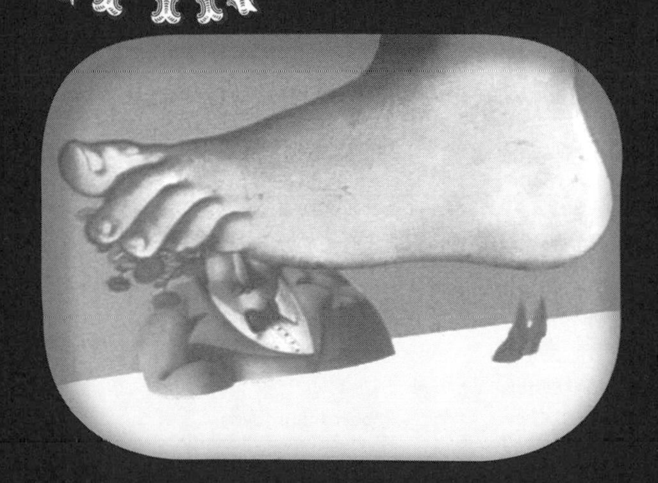

Marcia Landy

TV MILESTONES SERIES

Wayne State University Press Detroit

Copyright © 2005 by Wayne State University Press,
Detroit, Michigan 48201. All rights are reserved.
No part of this book may be reproduced without formal permission.
Manufactured in the United States of America.
09 08 07 06 05 5 4 3 2 1

Library of Congress Cataloging-in-Publication Data
Landy, Marcia, 1931–
Monty Python's flying circus / Marcia Landy.
p. cm. — (Contemporary approaches to film and television series. TV milestones)
Includes bibliographical references and index.
ISBN 0-8143-3103-3 (pbk. : alk. paper)
1. Monty Python's flying circus (Television program) I. Title. II. Series.

PN1992.77.M583L36 2005
791.45'72—dc22

2004020263

∞ The paper used in this publication meets the minimum requirements of the American National Standard for Information Sciences—Permanence of Paper for Printed Library Materials, ANSI Z39.48-1984.

CONTENTS

ACKNOWLEDGMENTS

I am grateful to Roger Saunders of Monty Python Pictures Ltd. for graciously granting me permission to reproduce video images from *Monty Python's Flying Circus* and to the Pythons for creating a thrilling moment in television history.

I am also indebted to Kirsten Strayer, graduate student in Film Studies at the University of Pittsburgh, and to Robert Mitchell of the University of Pittsburgh Center for Instructional Research and Development, who worked with me to prepare many of the images. My secretary, Carol Mysliwiec, was indefatigable in seeking sources for illustrations and in reproducing the many scripts for the shows. My graduate assistant, Ben Feldman, industriously located necessary articles and books on the Pythons, the British Broadcasting Corporation, and American and British reviews of the series, and Colin Brett provided me with helpful information on British television.

I also wish to express my gratitude to the various readers of the manuscript and to the editors of the TV Milestones Series, Barry Keith Grant and Jeannette Sloniowski, for their patient and critical reading of the work.

My special thanks to my friend and colleague Stanley Shostak for reading the manuscript countless times, for unweariedly discussing the form and content with me, and for encouraging me to clarify ideas.

I hope that the final form this book has taken repays his, the editors', and the outside readers' bountiful expenditure of time and effort.

The *Flying Circus* and the *Wide World of Entertainment*

In 1975, a compilation of episodes from *Monty Python's Flying Circus* was scheduled for broadcast on the American Broadcasting Company's (ABC) *Wide World of Entertainment*. The Pythons' American manager, Nancy Lewis, was verbally assured that episodes would be shown in their entirety. They were not. Entire segments were eliminated, and twenty-two minutes were excised to eliminate "offensive material," "strong language," and references to body parts that the Pythons often referred to as "naughty bits." The excisions, in keeping with the code of ABC's standards and networks practices, were based on "five categories of abomination: sexual allusiveness, general verbal misbehavior, fantasies of violence, offensiveness to particular groups, and scatology."[1]

Not only was the censored show unacceptable to the Pythons, but it was also totally "unfunny," even incoherent. Moreover, the group had to confront the prospect of one more episode scheduled for broadcast on ABC-TV. Unwilling to see their work mangled again, the Pythons attempted to block the next program, sending the following memo to the network: "We cannot state too strongly that this show is not Monty Python. Monty Python is the shows we made and edited. We want to do everything we can to stop them putting out another show like this."[2] Unfortunately, ABC declined to cancel the show, and the Pythons took the network to court for "copyright infringement" and "unfair competition against their uncut work."[3]

The Pythons did not lose completely, because ABC prefaced the contested program with an acknowledgment that the show was "edited by ABC." Furthermore, the judge, Morris E. Lasker, while granting concessions to ABC, asserted, "The law favors the proposition that a plaintiff has the right under ordinary circumstances to protection of the artistic integrity of his creation. In this case, I find that the plaintiffs have established an impairment to the integrity of their work."[4] The trial underscored differences between modes of producing commercial television in America as opposed to those in Britain: "Most people who work in [U.S.] television, particularly in commercial television, are prepared to accommodate themselves to the prevailing realities. The Pythons had the psychic and financial resources—and the safe shelter back home at the BBC—to enter the lists against Goliath. Few others do."[5]

Fortunately for television history, the *Flying Circus* provided audiences with a body of work that testifies to the creative potential of television. The dramatic court battle between ABC-TV and the Pythons exposed the constraints of television censorship as well as its consistent disregard for artistic integrity and ownership. However, the Pythons were able to transgress boundaries that most television, directly or even indirectly, avoided crossing, including nudity, explicit sexuality, fantasies of violence, and interdicted language—but not without incurring protests from pressure groups, politicians, and television administrators.

The *Flying Circus* was more than satire or parody of television. In its uses and abuses of television time, chronology, genres, and continuity, the four seasons of the show exposed both the existing limitations and the possibilities of the medium. The style of the *Flying Circus* and its choice of subjects for sketches revealed the potential of television to experiment with programming through format, character, visual image, and sound, outrageously exploiting the temporal nature of television through an appearance of immediacy, liveness, and experimentation with continuity as well as segmentation. The Pythons' self-reflexive and critical treatment of the character of television was evident through the constant interruptions in the comic segments, the linking of so many of the episodes to the British Broadcasting Corporation (BBC) setting, and the constant allusions to televisual modes of production and reception, alerting the spectator to how "the television image is held between innumerable institutions—of regulation, of the market-place, of expressed and inchoate opinion—and . . . offer[s] an ordering of things, even to exaggerate the chaos and orderlessness of things."[6]

The *Flying Circus* adopted a visual and verbal language that enabled transatlantic crossings in relation to questions of time, space, modes of narration, pastiche, and intertextuality. Specifically, the mixing of high and low culture, the intertextual dimension of the comic material, the daring treatment of the body and of sexuality, and the unrelenting critique of the television medium made the shows accessible to wide audiences despite the often erudite character of allusions to literature, philosophy, and history. The *Flying Circus* irreverently eschewed the conventions of situation comedy: the fully formed and coherent narrative script, stand-up routines, focus on a central individual, and decorum associated with the presentation not only of sexually explicit material but also of hallowed taboos concerning social institutions. In its style and subject matter, the *Flying Circus* experimented with a complex form of comedy that wreaked havoc not only with the TV apparatus but also with contemporary culture. This form of comedy, often identified as "stream of consciousness," "surreal," "nonsensical," or "carnivalesque," challenges logical categories and received conceptions of the world. In the Pythons' comedy, nonsense becomes a higher form of sense manifest through the language of the body, inversion of linguistic categories, and distortions in visual perception of places and events.

The Pythons

The first season of the *Flying Circus*, containing thirteen half-hour programs, began airing on BBC television on October 5, 1969. The second and third seasons also contained thirteen programs of the same length as the first, whereas the fourth contained only six programs, bringing the total of half-hour episodes to forty-five. The final program was aired on December 5, 1974.

Five Britons—John Cleese, Michael Palin, Terry Jones, Graham Chapman, and Eric Idle—and one American, Terry Gilliam, comprised the Python group. Though not usually designated as such, Carol Cleveland is deserving of recognition as the seventh Python. The show's producers were John Howard Davies and Ian MacNaughton. They also directed the series: Davies directed four of the first programs in 1969, and MacNaughton directed the remainder. Although the six Pythons worked collectively or in pairs on the scripts, other writers were occasionally hired for additional material (e.g., Douglas Adams and Neil Innes). Gilliam created the animation, and James Balfour, Alan Featherstone, Terry Hunt, Max Samett, and Stanley Spee were the cinematographers. Neil Innes was credited with musical direction (with uncredited assistance by Idle).

The *Flying Circus* underwent alterations during the four seasons as the Pythons experimented with the uses of comedy. The technique of abandoning punch lines and conclusions to various sketches and of moving more freely from sketch to sketch began during the middle of the first season. The Pythons' stream-of-consciousness style became more pronounced throughout the subsequent seasons. The motifs that characterized the sketches were as wide ranging as the style adopted to present them. The Pythons' forms of comedy tackled sexuality, law, medicine, politics, psychiatry, literary classics, comic books, language, cinema, and, above all, television. The steadily increasing popularity of the shows can be accounted for by the group's eclectic, daring, and innovative uses of the medium. However, after the second season, signs of restlessness were evident. Cleese appeared in fewer episodes and was absent from the fourth series. He later explained: "We were repeating ourselves. . . . If anyone did a sketch I could say, 'It's that sketch from the first series combined with that sketch from the second series.' Once you begin to identify sketches like that, I thought, why are we doing it?"[7] Despite his departure and the ending of the television series in 1974, the group (including Cleese) reunited for stage and television appearances and feature films.

The identity and success of *Monty Python's Flying Circus* was due in large measure to the similar cultural and social backgrounds of the individual Pythons. Also, they had prior and wide-ranging experience with writing and performing for stage, film, and television comedy (add to the mix Gilliam's work as an animator) before combining their talents in novel ways for television. An initial challenge they confronted in creating the show was the selection of a title. According to Roger Wilmut, "The team were anxious not to have a title which might give away the content of the show in any way."[8] Numerous titles were suggested—"Arthur Megapode's Flying Circus," "Owl Stretching Time," "Sex and Violence," "Gwen Dibley's Flying Circus," and so on—until the team finally decided on *Monty Python's Flying Circus*.

In the Pythons' experimentation with comedic form on the *Flying Circus*, no one individual was singled out—the men were collectively identified as "Monty Python." No one person was the "spokesperson," the "anchorman," or the "inspiration" for the series. An examination of the scripts, the acting roles assigned, and the synchronized performances of the group members reveals talents that are more generally distributed among the group according to their various talents. From initial discussions to script writing and from improvisation to rehearsals to shooting and to subsequent alterations prior to broadcasting, the Pythons (despite whatever personal animosities or annoyances they might have experienced) worked closely with one another. The cooperative character of their work was vastly enhanced by their shared histories due to their generation, social class, education, and intellectual predilections. They had had professional or academic careers in mind while at university, but they were also interested in writing and in selling their scripts to television, and they shared an eagerness to experiment with comedy through that medium.

All the men in the *Flying Circus* adopted drag during the course of the four seasons. As a group, the Pythons played "Pepperpots," "women on the street" and in the home (named and explained in the scripts, but not on the shows). They became the "Vox Pops," the voice of the people. The Pythons also masqueraded as "Gumbies" (named in the scripts but not in the performance), handkerchiefs tied around their heads, speaking as if their mouths are stuffed with cotton. Their various appearances were as witless psychiatrists, village idiots who profit by their inanity, bumbling and destructive flower arrangers, and conservative commentators on the state of society. Among their many personae, the Pythons also assumed the characters of small boys interviewed by announcers, lumberjacks, customers at a restaurant that serves only Spam as its fare, soldiers in World War I and II, inmates in a hospital to cure overacting, and old women—"Hell's Grannies"—who behave like members of a motorcycle gang.

John Cleese (b. 1939) was from a middle-class family and, after attending prep school, went to Cambridge University where he studied law. While at Cambridge, he joined the Footlights Club, a century-old university society, famous for its witty and satiric skits and revues. Commenting on the Footlights Club at the time he was a member, Cleese said that there was great variety, a wide cross-section of scientists, historians, and psychologists, in general "more of a mix of class."[9] His law career was short-circuited by a producer for the BBC, Peter Titheridge, who, in 1963, offered him a contract as a scriptwriter. In the years prior to the *Flying Circus*, Cleese wrote for and later appeared in a number of shows, significantly David Frost's television programs *That Was the Week That Was* (1962–63), *The Frost Report* (1966–67), and *At Last the 1948 Show* (1967). On these shows Cleese developed a comic style of looking absolutely normal—"like an accountant," as one critic described him—while doing and saying the most absurd things.

Cleese's success on the Frost shows led to his first film appearance in a small role in *Interlude* (1968) and in *The Bliss of Mrs. Blossom* (1968). On the *Flying Circus*, Cleese often (but not exclusively) played announcers, newsreaders, reporters, interviewers, and most memorably a victimized and outraged customer in the "Dead Parrot" sketch. Many *Flying Circus* fans also identify Cleese as the "Minister of Silly Walks" and as a "Gumby." He appeared in the third season in a variety of parts but did not appear in the fourth and final season of the show, though he remained with the group for recordings, stage shows, and several movies, including *Monty Python and the Holy Grail* (1975), *Monty Python's Life of Brian* (1979), and *Monty Python's The Meaning of Life* (1983). During the 1970s, he also appeared in such films as *The Best House in London* (1970), *The Rise and Rise of Michael Rimmer* (1970), *The Magic Christian* (1970), *The Statue* (1971), *The Love Ban* (1972), and *Romance with a Double Bass* (1972). Following his work on the *Flying Circus*, he also acted in a number of films, among which were *Time*

Bandits (1981), *Clockwise* (1986), *A Fish Called Wanda* (1988), *Erik the Viking* (1989), *Bullseye* (1991), *Splitting Heirs* (1993), *Mary Shelley's Frankenstein* (1994), and *The Out-of-Towners* (1999). In television, Cleese's most successful venture was *Fawlty Towers* (1975–79), considered by many to be one of the funniest and best-written situation comedies ever produced.

Michael Palin (b. 1943) read modern history at Oxford where he joined the equivalent of the Cambridge Footlights known as the Oxford Revue. There he met future Python Jones. The two found their vocation writing scripts for BBC-TV. Their *Do Not Adjust Your Set* (1967–69) and *The Complete and Utter History of Britain* (1969) were precursors to the *Flying Circus*. Palin, like the other Pythons, adopted a number of personae in the *Flying Circus*. His imitations of game show hosts and sports telecasters were played with oily familiarity and appropriately excessive energy. His versatile impressions also included prim housewives, wacky historical figures, dyslexic detectives, brash American-style announcers, tongue-tied television interviewers, gangsters,

John Cleese and Michael Palin as Gumby Psychiatrist and Patient

disorientated Spanish Inquisitioners, and bicycle repairmen. He has attributed the success of the *Flying Circus* to the similarity in cultural and social background of the Pythons: "We . . . all have similar sorts of education, and I think our parents were earning about the same amounts of money doing similar jobs . . . very middle. Terribly middle. Awfully middle."[10] He appeared in the various Monty Python films, and since the *Flying Circus*, Palin has acted in a number of films, most notably *Jabberwocky* (1976), *Time Bandits* (1981), *The Missionary* (1982; for which he wrote the script), *A Private Function* (1984), *A Fish Called Wanda* (1988), *American Friends* (1991), and *Fierce Creatures* (1997). He has also appeared on numerous television talk shows and travelogues and is the author of several books for children and one novel for adults.

Terry Jones (b. 1942) had aspired to be a poet and went on to the university with the idea of becoming an academic. Reading English at Oxford, however, confirmed Jones's conviction that he would rather create his own fictions and poetry than compose work about other writers. Like Palin and the other Pythons, Jones ended up writing television comedy. He collaborated with Palin on writing comedy sketches that the two sold to BBC-TV, in particular to the *David Frost Show* and to other programs such as *Do Not Adjust Your Set* (1967–69) and *The Complete and Utter History of Britain* (1969), both harbingers of *Flying Circus* sketches. Through writing and appearances on various television shows, he and Palin met the other future members of the Python group—Idle, Chapman, and Gilliam. On the *Flying Circus*, Jones played many of the memorable housewives and middle-aged, disgruntled maternal figures. He also appeared as a hustler, a naked organist, a salesman for such unusual types of candies as Crunchy Frog and Ram's Bladder Cup, a composer—Arthur "Two Sheds" Jackson—who in a television interview is never given the opportunity to speak about his music, one of the Spanish Inquisitioners, and in several striptease sketches. After the breakup of the group in 1975, Jones continued to collaborate with Palin in creating the BBC-TV's *Ripping Yarns* (1976–80). He has also been a codirector or director of such films as *Monty Python and the Holy Grail* (1975), *Monty Python's Life of Brian* (1979), *Monty Python's The Meaning of Life* (1983), *Personal Services* (1989), and *Erik the Viking* (1989).

Eric Idle (b. 1943) read English at Cambridge and became a member of the Footlights Club. He completed his degree in 1965 and joined *The Frost Report*, where he met and worked with the other future Pythons. As with the other members of the group, he was both writer and performer. Of the many character roles he assumed, Idle played the more "glamorous" females (including a judge in drag in the "Poofy Judges"). He also frequently assumed the role of the tiresome bore, as in the popular sketch "Nudge Nudge." In another sketch, he played a Native American in a theater waiting to see actress Cicely Courtneidge. When learning that she will not appear, he shoots arrows at members of the audience. He was the Python most associated with a focus, if not obsession, on the uses and abuse of language, in particular with verbal dyslexia. After the end of the *Flying Circus*, he continued to work on television projects. He did a couple of seasons for a BBC-2 program titled *Rutland Weekend Television* (1975–76), where he was able to draw on many motifs and techniques from the *Flying Circus*. In addition to appearing in films and on television, he has authored several books: *Hello Sailor* (1974), *The Rutland Dirty Weekend Book* (1976), the stage comedy *Pass the Butler* (1982), *The Quite Unusual Adventures of the Owl and the Pussycat: Based on the Poems, Drawings and Writings of Edward Lear* (1996), and *The Road to Mars: A Post-Modern Novel* (2000). His film credits include *The Adventures of Baron Münchausen* (1989), *Nuns on the Run* (1990), *Missing*

Pieces (1991), *Splitting Heirs* (1995), *Casper* (1995), *An Allan Smithee Film: Burn, Hollywood, Burn* (1997), *Quest for Camelot* (1998), and *Dudley Do-Right* (1999).

Tall, imposing, and authoritative-sounding Graham Chapman (b. 1941–d. 1989) played military officers and other figures of authority, along with his share of cross-dressing roles such as the Minister of Home Affairs, dressed in a frilly organza dress and unable to comment on the work of his ministry. He also appeared as bedraggled housewife Mrs. Premise to Cleese's Mrs. Conclusion in several sketches. Chapman had studied at Cambridge to prepare for a career in medicine but admitted in interviews that he was infected at a very young age by radio comedy, in particular *The Goon Show* (1951–60), a program that was to influence the Pythons' style. He was invited to become a member of the Footlights Club in his second year at Cambridge. Juggling between his commitment to medicine and his enchantment with comedic entertainment, Chapman dropped medicine. He went on a tour of New Zealand with the *Cambridge Circus* (derived from the Cambridge Footlights Revue) and chose comic

Idle as Quizmaster and Terry Jones as Karl Marx in "Communist Quiz"

entertainment as a career, appearing increasingly in television comedies that culminated in his role as regular writer and performer on the *Flying Circus*. Chapman appeared in and was responsible for cowriting the Python films in the years following the *Flying Circus*. His screen acting credits include such films as *Doctor in Trouble* (1970), *The Magic Christian* (1970), *The Rise and Rise of Michael Rimmer* (1970), *The Statue* (1971), *The Secret Policeman's Other Ball* (1982), and *Yellowbeard* (1983).

Terry Gilliam (b. 1940), the one American in the group, an artist in animation and an erstwhile scholar with an interest in physics and history, also found working on college humor more engaging than academic work. Before joining the Pythons, he had worked as a freelance illustrator for magazines. He was introduced to British television by Cleese. Gilliam is best remembered as the *Flying Circus'* wildly imaginative animator who presented images and vignettes of cannibalism, dismemberment, figures crushed by an oversized foot, catastrophes often culminating in explosions, mythical

Graham Chapman as a Hollywood director in "Twentieth Century Vole"

creatures, and labyrinthine and architectural images. His animation was not mere reinforcement or commentary on the sketches but served rather to create the fantastic, nonsensical, and surreal world that characterized the comic world of the Pythons. He also acted in episodes from time to time as, for example, Cardinal Fang in the Spanish Inquisition sketch. Most importantly, Gilliam's career led him to become a major film director known for such wildly imaginative works as *Time Bandits* (1981), *Brazil* (1985), *The Adventures of Baron Münchausen* (1989), *The Fisher King* (1991), *Twelve Monkeys* (1995), and *Fear and Loathing in Las Vegas* (1998).

There was a seventh Python. Carol Cleveland (b. 1943) was part of the *Flying Circus* since its inception, and her participation in episodes was critical to the success of the series. Her first appearance was as Mrs. Deirdre Pewtey in the "Marriage Guidance Counselor Sketch," where she seduces the marriage counselor. Her roles in the four seasons revealed her versatile comedic talents as a female seductress, proper lady of a manor, numerous secretaries, companion to Palin's

The *Flying Circus* logo

Lumberjack, and wife to Attila the Hun. According to Cleese, "Whenever we wanted someone who was a real woman, in the sense that sexually she was female and attractive, we asked Carol to do it."[11] Prior to her joining the *Flying Circus*, she had appeared on television in *Dixon of Dock Green* (1961), *The Avengers* (1961), and *The Saint* (1962). Along with her various television appearances and her roles in Python films, her film credits include *The Countess from Hong Kong* (1967), *All I Want Is You . . . and You . . . and You* (1974), *Vampira* (1974), *Return of the Pink Panther* (1975), *Brute* (1977), and *Half Moon Street* (1986).

The biographies of the Pythons reveal common interests and a style of expression that enabled the members to work as a unit and to be identified as a collective entity. The Pythons have asserted repeatedly that they rejected assigning themselves a representative to speak for the group. Unlike the fame associated with David Frost as personality and impresario, the group's celebrity status as performers on the *Flying Circus* was built on a collective star image—the Pythons, though fans may have their favorite episodes and performer (e.g., Cleese's "silly walk"). However, individual members of the *Flying Circus* have been singled out for attention and fame for their work in films and other television shows that they have directed or in which they have performed, particularly Cleese for his writing and performing on *Fawlty Towers* and Gilliam as a film director. The Pythons' composite identity can be attributed to their mode of collaboration in creating the show, the nature of their comedy, the protean roles they assumed in the various episodes, and the commonality of their backgrounds, which enabled them to address philosophical, political, and cultural concerns. The variety of the roles and the relative flexibility of each of the Pythons to shift into particular roles produced the combination of visual incongruity, verbal innuendo, vulgarity, and subtlety that reinforced the tendency of the *Flying Circus* to upset expectations.

The *Flying Circus* in a Changing British Culture

The specific cultural moment of the show's appearance was also intrinsic to its success. The particular irreverence and radical forms of the Pythons' performance on television flourished in the social and political climate of the 1960s and 1970s. This milieu was identified with youth, generational tensions, conflicting perceptions about the breaking up of national traditions and institutions, and the emergence of new forms of globalism via the commodities associated with popular culture, particularly fashion, music, tourism, and television. The character and effects of the *Flying Circus'* comedy are best described as belonging to this broadly acknowledged moment of transition.

The 1960s saw significant changes in British culture and politics that contributed to the emergence of groups such as the Pythons. What historian Tom Nairn has termed "the break-up of Britain" was characterized by a number of social and political changes that assisted in the transformation of Western Europe and the United Kingdom from a society of consensus to one of increasing, if not threatening, diversity.[12] It was a time of economic crisis resulting in the devaluation of the pound, strikes, disagreement over British entry into the European Economic Community, and rising demands for a limitation on immigration from Asia and Africa. The Labour government, in power from 1964 to 1970, also had to contend with rising demands for devolution from both Welsh and Scottish nationalists, to say nothing of demands for a withdrawal from Northern Ireland. There was growing disillusion with Labour and rising militancy, particularly by the Young Liberals who were demanding "withdrawal of all American troops from Vietnam; workers' control of nationalized industries; non-alignment in the Cold War; Britain's withdrawal from NATO; an end to the wage freeze; unconditional support for the 1965 seaman's strike; majority rule for Rhodesia; massive reductions in armaments; and entry into a Europe that would include the Communist bloc states of the East."[13]

This growing political instability had contradictory dimensions. Despite economic crises, there was a growth of personal income. More people owned their homes, cars, household appliances, and TV sets. This apparent affluence cloaked inequalities in wealth and economic opportunity.[14] The presumption of affluence that was to characterize British culture and society in the 1960s and 1970s was tied to the increasingly influential role of radio, cinema, and television. The "affluent society" as a phenomenon was directly and indirectly intertwined with media.

The 1960s and early 1970s, whether appropriately or not, were identified as a "countercultural moment." This counterculture was linked to youth, fashion, and rock and roll, with the Beatles at the center of this mass phenomenon, their performances producing frenzies akin to those demonstrated for Frank Sinatra and Elvis Presley. In 1966, the Beatles announced their retirement from public performing to concentrate on recording. In June 1967, this period reached a climax with the release of *Sgt. Pepper's Lonely Hearts Club Band*, an album greeted by young people internationally as evidence not only of the band's genius but also of the era's visionary hopes. While there was a working-class inflection to their image, in contrast to the middle-class Pythons, both groups—in their performances and in their reception—crossed over and challenged traditional borders of gender, race, and social class.

Elsewhere in the culture, the theater became a focal point of discontent through the plays and novels of John

Osborne and Kingsley Amis and productions by stage and film director Tony Richardson, a group identified as the Angry Young Men. Likewise, films challenged the class system, social institutions, family relations, and middle-class conformity as exemplified by the films directed by Lindsay Anderson (*This Sporting Life* [1963], *If . . .* [1968], *O Lucky Man* [1973]). The entertainment industry was enlivened by the entry of new talents from Oxford and Cambridge. Much of the wit and satire extended beyond the confines of academic life and was quite cognizant, if not affirming, of popular culture—its music, personalities, and movies. Signs of cultural transformation were evident in university revues such as the Cambridge Footlights Club and Oxford dramatic societies that were a training ground, not merely for future performers but also for politicians, cultural commentators, and academics.

The Footlights Club, in existence for nearly a century, was known for its spoofs on British society and university life. These revues of the 1960s, driven by a new generation of students, assumed a more daring satiric and countercultural edge. Surprisingly, this university background did not make the comedy parochial. Rather,

> the comedy produced by the Oxbridge generation succeeded in capturing audiences throughout the 1960s and early 1970s, at a time when education in general, and higher education in particular, was rapidly expanding in Britain. Nor is it an accident that the audience was a cult audience in many cases, and relatively young. It was an audience that shared the culture (and attitudes to the culture) of the writers and performers themselves.[15]

Shows such as *Beyond the Fringe* (1961–64) and *Cambridge Circus* (1963–64) traveled beyond the university into national and international theater and media. Writers and performers such as Alan Bennett, Peter Cook, Jonathan Miller, and Dudley Moore became well known for their satiric treatment of politics and culture. The successful transition of these individuals from university into mass media was, of course, facilitated by "old school ties," but it was also dependent on their daring experimental energies.

The counterculture of the 1960s and 1970s was also tied to the dissemination of images associated with "Swinging London." The popularity of "Swinging London" was associated with live rock group performances and gaudy album covers expressing a keen attention to bodily appearance, "mod" fashion, and miniskirts, and these new images of British life were further associated with youth, popular music, and cinema. Pop musicals such as those made by Richard Lester and featuring the Beatles (*A Hard Day's Night* [1964], *Help* [1965]), as well as New Wave films identified with "Swinging London," made their own contribution to the culture of the time. New stars appeared such as Julie Christie, whose *Darling* (1965) set the images and tone for the media-driven 1960s, increasingly identified with global capital and the focus on the consumption of commodities.

The visual styles of such films as *The Knack* (1965), *Morgan* (1966), *Georgy Girl* (1966), and *Alfie* (1966) offered vital and attractive images of youth culture, generational differences, music, street life, and antiestablishment attitudes. However, such films as Richard Lester's two Beatles' films displayed critical attitudes toward British cinema and society. These films provided the illusion that Britain had crossed over into international filmmaking by capitalizing on the popularity of the Beatles, their youthful images, their music, and their working-class savvy. Their form of comedy was in many ways anticipatory of the Pythons', a humor inflected with surrealism, "performed in a deadpan manner," and conveying "a sense of knowingness about their predicament as pop stars who were answerable to an insatiable media."[16]

By the 1960s, television had become an established part of the world of spectacle and information. Despite the fact that BBC television production was still imbued with a belief in the efficacy of information as a recording of "reality," significant changes in format began to occur with the entry of new personalities and new styles into television. The Pythons were part of worldwide cultural transformations that increasingly challenged existing social and political institutions, opening the door, for better or worse, to more critical, and perhaps cynical, approaches to questions of authority, gender, generation, sexuality, and national and regional identity.

The British Broadcasting Corporation

The style and motifs of the *Flying Circus* are closely tied to the changing character of the BBC during the 1960s, its "increasing break away from the cosy image of the 1950s."[17] The BBC had long been a major influence in the development of radio and television not only in the United Kingdom but worldwide. For example, cultural critic Edward Said wrote,

> I remember . . . as a boy growing up in the Arab world, where the BBC was an important part of our life; even today phrases like "London said this morning" are a common refrain in the Middle East. They are always used with the assumption that "London" tells the truth. Whether this view of the BBC is only a vestige of colonialism I cannot tell, yet it is also true that in England and abroad the BBC has a position in public life enjoyed neither by gov-

ernment agencies like the Voice of America nor by the American networks, including CNN.[18]

This august image of the BBC was often a target of Python comedy and has its roots in the history of the broadcasting entity. The BBC was established as a private company in 1922, but by 1927, it had become a public institution. Under the directorship of John Reith, the BBC evolved its identity as a "public service" institution, connecting mass cultural uplift and enlightenment in the tradition of Matthew Arnold. Reith, a proselytizer for moral and educational uplift, believed "that the education and moral uplift of the public was the real purpose of radio, but carefully selected entertainment was an acceptable means for carrying out the task. The BBC used every opportunity to establish standards of every kind in the minds of listeners: in guiding, for example, the pronunciation of the English language and in attempting to create a more enlightened electorate."[19] This notion of public service guided the BBC through the years of World War II, organizing the system of administration for the corporation, setting standards of behavior, and determining relations between it and Parliament. Reith regarded the BBC as independent of political control, yet this independence was largely a myth, because the corporation was closely tied ideologically and materially to the state. In fact, the BBC as a servant of the nation was expected to communicate the highest ideals of a unified culture.

BBC's television approach was inherited from BBC radio[20] and manifested in the philosophy of BBC administration, in the types of personnel employed by the BBC, and in the programming that guided the corporation through World War II. One of the major transformations in the televisual medium was occasioned by the breakup of the BBC monopoly in the establishment of the commercial ITV network in 1955 under the aegis of the Independent Television Authority (ITA) mandated by the Television Act of 1954. As a consequence of the breakup of its monopoly, the BBC underwent significant changes in its structure to compete with commercial broadcasting while maintaining its tradition of quality. Challenges to public service broadcasting were evident in the changing administrative and programming structure of the organization. "As long as it was the only broadcaster in the country, it could do as it liked. . . . Now it competes in a marketplace, though without being driven by the commercial imperatives of the market; and it has to chase viewers and listeners, though without making money from them; most of its income derives from the license fees levied on television sets whether the owners watch the BBC or not."[21] The corporation entered into competition for personnel, time slots, and programming involving talks and current affairs, drama, and light entertainment. From the late 1960s to the 1970s, the BBC offered news and public affairs; special nonfiction features; educational programs; art shows involving painting, music, and theater; television dramas; films; sports; and light entertainment (e.g., comedy specials, sitcoms, variety shows, talk shows, quiz shows, etc.). For example, a fair share of the programming in the late 1960s and 1970s involved a mixture of drama, melodramas and comedies, series and individual theatrical performances, early British, American, and European films, news programs, documentaries, biographies, history programs, interviews with celebrities, debates on current issues, and talk shows. Significantly, the *Flying Circus* addressed the increasingly diverse character of television programming in its sketches by turning its comic focus on news, reportage, interviews, game shows, sitcoms, children's shows, plays, and films.

Television in the 1960s also saw the emergence of new personalities and new programming formats, the most notable being *That Was the Week That Was* (TW3) and *The Frost Report*, for which future Pythons wrote. The medium was in the process of conceding to new generational and cultural forces. Among the new faces, David Frost set the standard for a form of variety show, including news reportage, political lampooning, interviews, and comic skits that introduced and showcased major comedic talents. Frost's contributions to television were organizational: "[He] had an amazing gift for putting a sketch together so that it worked on the air."[22]

TW3 became known for its uses of music, topicality, sketches, political lampooning, churchmen, and scandals such as the Profumo affair, which ultimately brought down the Macmillan government.[23] Such shows as *TW3* used scandals against the establishment as a means to broaden "the range of acceptable vocabulary on TV."[24] However, Frost claimed, "We did not come to *TW3* with a specific agenda or political program. We were not a further example of what the newspapers called 'The Angry Young Men.' We were the Exasperated Young Men—exasperated by Britain's recurring failures, by hypocrisy and complacency, and by the shabbiness of its politics."[25]

According to Frost, the much-vaunted cultural and political changes were "superficial rather than fundamental," and the objective of *TW3* was rather to "decode some of our customs, attitudes and behavior."[26] Frost was influential in encouraging new styles of British television, and he was also instrumental in advancing the careers of some of the Pythons, introducing new personalities and through them bringing innovation into television programming. He became an international personality and moved easily back and forth from the United Kingdom to the United States to the European continent, thus confirming the international character of television. In 1967, *The Frost Report* and the *At Last the 1948 Show* (1967) featured Cleese and Chapman, soon to be of the *Flying Circus*. The *At Last the 1948 Show* provided some indication of the direction of the *Flying*

Circus in its lampooning of television and its occasional recourse to loosely structured sketches, although the Pythons were eventually to develop their comic style much further. The flamboyant and impudent style of the *Flying Circus* was the recipient of opportunities offered by the BBC at a critical moment in its history.[27] The character of the *Flying Circus* derived in large part from the fact that the shows appeared during a transitional moment in British media culture, challenging both the public service legacy of BBC programming and commercial television.

During the first season of the *Flying Circus*, the group experienced minimal opposition to the subject matter or language of the shows. When first embarking on the *Flying Circus*, the Pythons were told at the BBC, "Do whatever you like. Within reason, as long as it's within the bounds of common law." Increasingly, public pressure groups, politicians, and BBC administrators mounted opposition. Although "it is the proud claim of the BBC that for the Corporation, censorship does not exist,"[28] indirect or self-censorship was expected and practiced. Given the transgressive dimensions of the series in relation to sexually explicit material and language, pressure for censorship was beginning to appear by 1971.

"Moral majority" groups such as Mary Whitehouse's National Viewers and Listeners Association mounted opposition to the program. The Pythons antagonized vocal conservative and fundamentalist constituencies that were part of the growing backlash against the "permissive" society. Increasingly, the series had to confront challenges from conservative social groups in Britain in the form of complaints to the BBC and government politicians through vitriolic letters, organized public meetings, and appearances on talk shows, but the Pythons found ways to address their critics' complaints by incorporating their opponents' objections into the comic material of the *Flying Circus* through the role of the "Vox Pops" (the people's voice). Dissenting points of view were also incorporated into the shows by means of Python-created letters that were televised and read aloud, expressing outrage over certain sketches. Or members of the group (often Chapman) as themselves or in one of their comic personae would break off a skit and express disgust over alleged obscenity or bad taste.

Organized opposition to the show, familiar in the wake of reactions to the counterculture and oppositional politics of the 1960s and 1970s, was to have the effect of generating more surveillance on the part of the corporation, so that BBC authorities began to take "greater interest in programming before a show was broadcast."[29] For instance, the head of light entertainment, concerned about indecorous language usage, asked the Pythons, "Do you have to use the word 'bastard' twice?"[30] There was also the case of administrative attempts to cut such words as *wee wee, masturbation*, and *bugger* as well as certain animated images that were construed as "obscene": for example, the "complaints about 'the big penis' that comes through the door—in fact, a 'severed arm' in a skit involving Oscar Wilde."[31]

The *Flying Circus* had also to contend with being scheduled into unpopular and often late-hour time slots (eleven at night on Sundays for Series One), where it was supplanted by regional programming. According to Wilmut, "Most regions opted out for their own late-night programming; most regions never saw it at all, one or two just saw the odd program, and Scotland saw it on different nights. It was only when the series was repeated that the regions were able to see what they had been missing."[32] Later the program was aired at a more regular time—10:15 PM on Tuesdays for Series Two and 10:15 PM on Thursdays for Series Three. The fourth and final season of the show was scheduled for Thursdays at 9 PM. The treatment by the higher echelons of BBC indicated administrative uneasiness about the show, but despite these conflicts the *Flying Circus* increased its audience and extended its popularity beyond national boundaries.

The Pythons and American Television

Monty Python's Flying Circus represents a significant moment in the study of the crossover from British to American television, but, as J. S. Miller in his discussion of connections between British television and American culture writes, the 1950s had already paved the way for British imports: "One might plausibly chart the beginning of the British relationship with American television from the coronation of Queen Elizabeth on June 2, 1953."[33] The appearance of British films on American television constituted a "British ur-invasion in which as much as 25 per cent of the feature films presented on American televisions during the period 1948–1952 were British in origin."[34] In the 1960s, such shows as *Danger Man* (1960–61, 1964–67), *The Saint* (1962–69), *The Prisoner* (1967–68), and *The Avengers* (1961–69), capitalizing on the Bond phenomenon, constituted another, more substantial second wave of British infiltration, influencing the character of American spy serials.

With the advent of U.S. public television in the 1960s, "heritage" programming entered the U.S. television world through *Masterpiece Theatre* (1971–present) and the many canonical literary works it introduced. The appearance of Alistair Cooke as host on the omnibus show enhanced an image of urbane British culture so popular with American audiences. Satiric revues also crossed the Atlantic. *TW3*, tailored for U.S. audiences, appeared in the mid-1960s, drawing also on the talents of British performers, most notably David Frost. *TW3* appeared on NBC in 1964–65 and was "subsequently [to] become a symbol of the 1960s as a decade,"[35] influential on both sides of the Atlantic.

The *Flying Circus* first appeared on North American television in 1970 when the Canadian Broadcasting Corporation

(CBC) aired some sketches. The show became known in the United States when station KERA in Dallas broadcast it in 1974 and 1975, and further broadcasts appeared on WNET in New York. Along with such shows as *Masterpiece Theatre* and *Upstairs Downstairs* (1971–75), the *Flying Circus* was circulated through public television. By 1975, some 131 stations were broadcasting the *Flying Circus.*[36] The Pythons had already made stage appearances in the United States, but it was the compilation film *And Now for Something Completely Different* (1971) that brought the Pythons' style of comedy to popular attention. The Pythons were also invited to appear on the *Tonight Show*. According to Python critic Roger Wilmut, "Many young Americans saw it [the *Flying Circus*] and believed in it to the extent of its becoming a campus cult."[37] The term "cult" suggests a particular type of devoted, collective, and intense emotional reaction usually associated with fandom. The *Flying Circus* appealed to young people and to disaffected groups for its irreverence toward authority and for its unconventional uses of television—it exposed the existence of deeply felt desires for alternatives to social and cultural conformity in the United Kingdom, America, and elsewhere.

The ability of the *Flying Circus* to cross national boundaries is due in large part to the character and evolution of the television medium and its technological capacity to reach all quarters of the world. This capacity of television (or at least certain events and forms of entertainment) to cross national boundaries is, in the case of the *Flying Circus*, due also to its atypical comic format. Not only did the *Flying Circus* become trendy, if not fashionable, in America, its popularity continued to grow in Germany. It was also popular in Japan, where humor in the Python vein appeared to be "fairly earthy and occasionally savage."[38]

The *Flying Circus* can be said to resemble such U.S. television network programs as *Laugh-In* (1968–73) and *Saturday*

Night Live (1975–present), because these shows were based on sketches, vignettes, slapstick, personalities, and topical allusions. Yet the differences between the U.S. shows and the *Flying Circus* are instructive for understanding the Pythons' innovative approaches to television comedy. *Laugh-In* relied on specific caricatures (the sneaky German; the zany blonde; the wild, out of control female) and the continuity of the two hosts (Rowan and Martin), who constituted "normality" in the midst of the apparent bedlam created by the other characters. In contrast, the Pythons kept their audiences off balance. Not only did they alternate roles and introduce abundant critical references to the television medium, but their carnivalesque comedy challenged in accessible ways reigning values and beliefs concerning madness and sanity.

What finally differentiated the *Flying Circus* was that it was not like television (at least not dominant television) but more "like a comic zany novel than what we normally associate with television comedy."[39] This comparison with the comic novel characterizes the unpredictable and unconventional character of the overall structure of the *Flying Circus* and the protean roles of each of the Pythons. The Pythons' comedy has been linked to Bakhtin's conception of the carnivalesque, with its discontinuous, grotesque, and ambivalent style.[40] In particular, as delineated by Bakhtin, the comedy associated with the carnivalesque is linked to popular art. It is correlated with bodily functions that cannot or refuse to accept official constraints and identified with animality, irreverence in behavior and action, alterations in size and perspective, and forms of language that disrupt reason and meaning and challenge both common and good sense.[41] In effect, the carnival is a grotesque and disorderly vision of the world turned upside down, where everything is inverted and altered, but where nonsense reveals the tension between chaos and stability.

While the episodes in the series might appear chaotic from a formal perspective, what provided coherence was a monstrous (and philosophic) vision of the world that defied the clichés and platitudes of social life as represented by the common sense of the culture. American television seems reliant on personalities, on exposé, on oblique critiques—if they exist at all—of timely political and social topics, and above all, on different conceptions of the level of intelligence and tolerance of the viewing audience. The Pythons' type of experimentation was at odds with the needs of commercial television to satisfy sponsors, the direct and indirect forms of censorship, and concerns about ratings. In short, the philosophy of the BBC world inhabited by the Pythons and that of the major networks of American television tended to utilize the medium differently.

As critic Anna Mulrine writes, "They [the Pythons] were saying stuff that would get you smacked if you said it in school."[42] They introduced subjects that were hardly obscure to viewers across national boundaries: marriage fatigue; same-sex bias; middle-class pretensions concerning culture; the banal, repetitive, even exploitative character of much media (film and television); and the pretensions of high culture. This "something different" style yet familiar subject matter enabled the *Flying Circus* to appeal to American audiences. The transnational popularity of the *Flying Circus* profited from the association of the Pythons with the rock groups of the 1960s and 1970s. In fact, Nancy Lewis, the rock-and-roll press agent responsible for bringing the group to U.S. television, marketed the Pythons as a rock band, and this type of promotion paid off. Comparing the "Pythons" or "Flying Circus" (not merely because of the name) to a rock group was appropriate. In a sense, the Pythons became the Beatles of comedy—youthful and exuberant, violating norms, experimenting with media, and introducing new forms and styles.

One cannot claim that appeal for the *Flying Circus* in the United States reached the height of such classic U.S. television shows as *I Love Lucy* (1951–56), *Gunsmoke* (1955–75), and *M*A*S*H* (1972–83). And the *Flying Circus* also had its detractors; not everyone appreciated the importation of the show to the United States. Some critics, such as Cleveland Amory, found it too juvenile and overlong: "Everything is done at least twice—and heavily."[43] The *Flying Circus* appealed more to university-educated, increasingly younger audiences and to the culturally disaffected.

In accounting for the positive reception of the series in the United States in 1975, one reviewer wrote, "Monty Python cultists—like the big-city midnight movie cultists—seem to regard the program as camp, that which tests the values of traditional entertainment by converting 'bad' into 'so-bad-it's good.'"[44] "Camp" is identified with "bad taste," the violation of aesthetic norms of judgment often as an end in itself. While there may be those critics who regard the *Flying Circus* as camp and ascribe its appeal to its "bad taste," this view ignores the cultural and intellectual importance of the Python form of comedy. The Pythons' uses of nudity, references to "naughty bits," and drag challenged socially sanctioned forms of language and behavior.

To reduce the appeal of the series to its camp and cultic character is another way of consigning the series to vogue rather than to critical reflection. While camp qualities (e.g., excessive artifice and theatricality often associated with gender and sexuality) may account for its popularity among certain audiences, they do not adequately address the multifaceted and complex character of the series' challenges to contemporary culture and politics. The Cuban missile crisis, the Kennedy assassination, the increasing involvement in Vietnam and the growing protests against this policy, the rise of the Yippies and the Black Panthers, the assassination of Dr. Martin Luther King Jr., and the Watts riots, among other national and international events, contributed to popular uneasiness about foreign and domestic policy, an unrest identified with universities and with absurdist comedians such as Lenny Bruce. Python cultural politics played on the absurdity and abuses in language, social institutions, and media.

Television played a major role in disseminating politics through its news, "specials," and talk shows. Judging by the content and form of many of the Python sketches, the series was acutely conscious of television as a perpetrator of misinformation. The Pythons repeatedly violated conventional behaviors associated with sexuality, gender, and ethnicity and made fun of television genres developed to circulate data (news, lectures, interviews, quiz shows, etc.). In their unsettling uses of comedy, the *Flying Circus* highlighted the global role of information and spectacle that was to become increasingly more pervasive in the last decades of the twentieth century. The wide appeal of the series, however, extends beyond its critical/intellectual focus on television: it also exploited fundamental aspects of comedy derived from drama, literature, and cinema.

Antecedents and Influences

The comedy of the *Flying Circus*, although distinctive, did not arise by spontaneous generation: it had important antecedents in the music hall and in British cinema. The series relied on existing forms of British comedy but molded these forms to its own ends. The Pythons were not polemic or partisan. For the most part, they did not create and perform direct and topical political satire. The targets of their humor came from all levels of society, from different classes and different political positions, though their subject matter and treatment were largely geared toward educated and middle-class audiences. Their comedy addressed domestic life, work, leisure, political practices, education, high and popular art forms, religion, sexuality, social class, gender, and the cultural forms in which these institutions and practices were articulated and disseminated.

By means of a vast, encyclopedic engagement with drama, literature (e.g., Shakespeare, Dickens), movies (Hitchcock, Kubrick, Peckinpah), philosophy (Sartre, Kierkegaard), popular music, painting, and forms of television, the *Flying Circus*' multifaceted comedy addressed pervasive traditional cultural forms and values, punctuating and dramatizing dominant modes of confronting the practices of contemporary society often filtered through the focus on the televisual medium. Attentive to the complex issue of how language, and especially television language, functioned to create and sustain social issues, the *Flying Circus* portrayed, dissected, and destabilized conventions, formulas, and clichés in unprecedented fashion.

The *Flying Circus* was not a serial drama such as *Upstairs Downstairs*. It was not a variety show, featuring different performers, although occasionally personalities appeared in sketches and musical performances were introduced. Nor could the show be properly identified as satire, though there were satirical elements in the sketches:

> The Pythons were trying to resist what is usually meant by satire. . . . Monty Python was more interested in a truth that satirists hate to think about: people don't want to change their minds and rarely change them in response to the lessons of satire. It's hard to face this without getting cynical. Positively embracing it is the heart of the Pythons' style. Renouncing satire's ineffectual upper hand, they took all their knowledge and redistributed it across the board, so you can never tell which character will know what.[45]

Disclaimers notwithstanding, the *Flying Circus* exemplifies two strategies characteristic of satire described by

Northrop Frye: "One is wit or humor founded on fantasy or a sense of the grotesque or the absurd, the other is an object of attack."[46] The grotesque quality of the characters and the situations into which they are placed in the *Flying Circus* rely on "an imaginative playing with the forbidden or the inexpressible."[47] Humans are reduced to automata by highlighting eccentric, out of the ordinary, and bizarre situations, invoking physical and psychic "deviations" from socially sanctioned behavior. The satiric "object of attack" in the *Flying Circus* covers a range of types identified with Menippean satire: "pedants, bigots, cranks, virtuosi, enthusiasts, rapacious and incompetent professional men of all kinds."[48]

The innovativeness of the Pythons, while attacking most everything that was socially and culturally venerated, was not tendentious. Python Idle said,

> Comedy's job is to be against things, not for them. Monty Python was firmly apolitical, though anti-authoritarian in flavour. In the years in which it flourished it was no longer possible to take any party seriously. Thus, the Python attack is fixed on all authority figures involved in growing up in this country: teachers, policemen, judges, mothers, minor royalties, politicians, army officers, even those in charge of the BBC; and it consequently aroused the anger of the middle classes.[49]

Following this general disavowal of partisan politics, a fruitful direction in identifying the comic forms of the series resides in what has commonly been labeled "anarchic" and "surreal." This anarchic dimension involved an unsettling of social conventions through cross-dressing and gags that lacked the restrained decorum concerning sexuality, fetishism, "perversion" (including cannibalism), bureaucracy, family, work, and animality. A quarter of a century later, though some of the topical allusions may be lost, the sharp edge of the Pythons' comedy remains cogent in their invocation and self-conscious treatment of popular culture (silent and sound cinema, vaudeville, music hall, and clowning) that calls attention to the showmanship of the performers.

Predecessors to the carnivalesque dimensions of the *Flying Circus* can be found in British film comedy. For example, the *Carry On* films, produced from the late 1950s to the 1970s, offered a ribald, earthy form of humor and identified with a repertory group of actors (Charles Hawtry, Joan Sims, Kenneth Williams, Sid James, and Hattie Jacques) who tackled in satiric and slapstick fashion revered British institutions—the army, the medical profession, classical history, patriotism, leisure life, and sports. The *Carry On* series also spoofed genre forms—empire films, medical melodramas, and historical films. Many of the objections raised against the Pythons might well have been invoked against the *Carry On* series.[50]

In the case of the *Carry On* films, there was a looseness of narrative structure, strings of unrelated and physically pointed gags, a focus on institutions and a bawdy emphasis on gender and class stereotypes, "a consistent refusal of the realism of character acting," and the "insertion of already familiar, usually crude jokes."[51] Both the *Carry On* films and the *Flying Circus* treated the high seriousness of social institutions in irreverent fashion. Also like the *Carry On* films, the Python comedy relied on direct address to the audience, often calling attention to the absurdity of the actions performed and to the artifice of the medium. The endless running gags, the punning, and the undressing of hallowed rituals were central to both *Carry On* and Python comedy.

Beyond comparisons in subject matter, institutional derision, and sexual innuendo, the *Carry On* series and the *Flying Circus* part company. The *Flying Circus* had little investment in consistent narratives and was blunter about its sexual transgressions, introducing frequent cross-dressing, sexually laden double entendres, and a form of comedy that was dispersive, unruly, and discontinuous. Aside from the centrality of its focus on the forms, languages, and personalities of television, the *Flying Circus* went in a more overtly critical direction, in its outspoken and daring treatment of sexuality, particularly gay sexuality, its insistence on the manifold public and private expressions of power and domination, and its challenge to both canonical and mass cultures. In short, the Pythons' humor differed significantly from the populist, working-class traditions of the *Carry On* films.

The *Flying Circus* is indebted as well to BBC radio comedy and particularly to the *Goon Show* (1951–60, original title: *Crazy People*), which ran for almost a decade and featured the talents of Spike Milligan, Harry Secombe, and Peter Sellers. Milligan, however, was the dominant figure in the group. This show has been described as an "anarchic mixture of nonsensical character, banterist wordplay, and weird sound effects, all pitched at high speed."[52] The *Goon Show*, with its dizzying pace, its irreverence for social and broadcasting conventions, its play with verbal language, and its episodic, discontinuous character, was often described, in terms applicable to the *Flying Circus*, as surrealist, outrageous, and unpredictable, and it featured a range of characters with such names as Bluebottle, Ned Seagoon, Major Denis Bloodnok, Eccles, Gryprype-Thynne, Count Jim Moriarty, and Henry Crun.

The Pythons' sketches that focus on BBC programming and, more broadly, on the character of popular culture and contemporary social life, were indebted to the *Goon Show* and the antics of Milligan. Above all, the quality of the Python humor relied on the appearance of spontaneity and of liveness and on an image of the world turned upside down. However, the comedy of the *Flying Circus* ultimately veered in another direction. Where the *Goon Show* "brought situations to their illogical conclusion," the *Flying Circus* took "ideas to their logical conclusion, and then beyond that for a considerable way."[53] In its focus on the impure and mutable body, on violence and death, and on the coextensiveness of sense and nonsense, the Python world unsettled commonsense conceptions of language and action by inviting the viewer to contemplate and participate in how meaning is made and possibly unmade. The carnivalesque character of the *Flying Circus* implicated both the Pythons and their audiences in a complex celebration and critique of culture and politics that transcended, if not altered, national forms of comedy.

Situating Comedy

The *Flying Circus* struck at the heart of what certain critics have termed postmodernity via the "society of the spectacle," where the image and the sound byte reign and are seemingly unchallenged by "reality."[54] This is a world where "distance is abolished in all things: between the sexes, between opposite poles, stage and auditorium, between the protagonists of action, between subject and object, between the real and its double."[55] However, while Python comedy, especially in its focus on media, appears to blur taken-for-granted and binary distinctions between the real and the imaginary, in fact the series did not do away with distinctions between fiction and fact, truth and falsity, and body and mind, but, in the spirit of the carnivalesque, produced a chaotic world that made such distinctions suspect.

The Pythons' dreamlike uses of animation, their protean uses of themselves and the forms they adopted for addressing the spectator, their play with language as nonsense, and their self-conscious references to the medium of television not only challenged accepted representations of the world but constituted a profound investigation of the medium as serving to mystify the matter of images. The comedy thrives on direct address, de-familiarization through undermining narrative expectations, discontinuities in space and time, reversals of physical and social characteristics, and the emptying of generic forms. Thus, rather than affirming the postmodern condition, the Python comedy serves as a means of dramatizing and questioning ways of seeing and believing.

The persona of the Pythons is central to their comedy, and they address the audience directly through both their various character roles and as themselves. Direct address or its semblance is crucial to many forms of comedy, and so it is with the *Flying Circus*. As Steve Neale and Frank Krutnik write, "Direct address to camera (in the form of a look and/or comment) and references to the fiction are just two of the most obvious—and obviously transgressive—devices used very frequently in comedies to draw attention to their artifice, to highlight the rules by which it is governed and to raise a laugh."[56] Direct address in the *Flying Circus* often entails episodes in which one of the Pythons as himself, or through a persona, comments on the bad taste of a sketch or on its lack of humor.

Another related form of de-familiarization in the *Flying Circus* involves drawing attention to the sketch in the process of its production for television. The sketches are often interrupted by the introduction of letters of complaint, the uses of voice-over, the recurrent and disruptive materialization of a man in armor, the transition from studio shots to animation, or the insertion of a segment from an earlier sketch. In "Yprès, 1914," a historical sketch on World War I to be performed for television, a floor manager interrupts the action to remove "anyone not involved in this scene." No sooner does he leave and the sketch resumes than he appears again to complain of a changed caption. After portraying the forcible removal of a man with a space suit who is obviously out of place, the sketch is again interrupted by an abrupt cut to Karl Marx embracing Che Guevara. The return to the "Communist

Quiz" sketch is an instance of the hybrid, nonlinear, and unpredictable character of the shows, disrupting expectations of narrative continuity, underscoring the arbitrariness of narration, and highlighting the irreverent treatment of cultural icons by situating them incongruously within a game show context rather than in a news format.

One of the most recurrent comic devices employed by the *Flying Circus* is the inversion of conventional social images, involving the undermining of generational, gendered, class, and sexual images. Python critic Roger Wilmut has termed the sketches in which such inversions occur as "reversal sketches." These sketches function by means of placing an unpredictable character in a predictable situation. For example, in "Hell's Grannies," a sketch ostensibly involving news reportage on crime, the rebellious criminals are not young men but old women dressed in leather, creating havoc on motorcycles, robbing, stealing, and assaulting people on the street.

In the format sketch, conventional styles of representation were "emptied" and replaced "with something ludicrous,"[57] as in the numerous sketches that draw on Shakespearian plays, popular films, and television programming. The BBC has its share of "educational" programs involving informative discussions of the work of specific artists. In one instance of the format sketch, "The Poet McTeagle," the Pythons present a profile of the work of a fictitious contemporary poet, Ian McTeagle, by following the typical format of this type of program and replacing it with a completely different context through altering viewers' expectations of a character or a situation. Instead of being presented with an exalted image of a great poet, the Python viewer is given a portrait of a banal character. Poet McTeagle's "greatest" lines, cited several times throughout the skit, are "Lend us a couple of bob 'til Thursday. I'm absolutely skint. But I'm expecting a postal order and I can pay you back as soon as it comes." Rather than focusing on the "creative" dimensions of poetry, the skit draws on the tendency to celebrate national identities, the propensity toward banality in much "celebrated" poetry, and the pompous tendency of television presenters to inflate artistic work and the figure of the artist, and to ignore, whenever possible, any exploration of an artist's work.

In a sketch focusing on BBC programming, "The Role of the Nude in Art," the viewer might anticipate a lecture by a noted authority on the arts whereby the audience is initiated into the regions of high culture (e.g., Sir Kenneth Clark on art on the BBC). In this sketch, Palin completely overturns the high seriousness and educational function of this type of television lecture. In his lecture, he cannot restrain his tendency to make verbal "slips." Beginning with a conventional introduction to the subject of art history, he says, "I would like to talk to you tonight about the nude," and then adds, to his dismay, "in my bed." He continues, "In the history of—my bed—Art, Art. The history of Art. The nude in the history of—tart. Call girl. I'll start again." The intro-

World War I in "Yprès, 1914"

duction of sex through the insistent intrusion of the lecturer's unconscious disrupts the automatic character of media discourse, exposing the libido of the commentator and contaminating inflated and circumlocutious intellectual discourse by injecting bedroom politics.

The Pythons' self-reflexivity combines "a comic foregrounding of the conventions of television, with a comic foregrounding of the conventions of comic forms themselves. It is this *combination* that produces the particular density of construction and self-reference that constitutes the hallmark of that style."[58] In the spirit of what some critics have termed the "postmodern" character of the *Flying Circus*, the comedy sketches created a pastiche of an absurd world, one that subsumed the particular obsessions, partial truths, zealousness, misdirected seriousness, and aporias of middle and working-class existence.

The Pythons' carnivalesque humor in the *Flying Circus* relied on deflating every sentiment, every heroic gesture, and every style that served to enhance and to maintain socially sanctioned values and behavior. The comic devices of the *Flying Circus* were an encyclopedia of comedy—involving gags, slapstick, the grotesque, wordplay, and banter—with the goal of producing a familiar world, rendering it strange, but ultimately and paradoxically making it recognizable. The *Flying Circus*, in its uses of image and sound, undermining of traditional forms of storytelling, and profligate uses of time, constitutes a complex assault on a society in which television is a prime instrument of communication and a barometer of contemporary culture while using the very medium of television to perform this critique.

Television Time

Beyond the Pythons' explorations of the various forms of programming, the overall form of the series is connected to the basic attributes of television—segmentation and flow. Drawing on and utilizing every available genre—news, interviews, game shows, commercials, and films on television, the *Flying Circus* capitalized on and exploited the segmented character of television time. However, in its profligate "waste" of time through the disavowal, interruption, repetition, and lack of closure of many sketches, the *Flying Circus* calls attention to the continuous and indiscriminate character of time inherent in the televisual. While individual programs have their time slots and are self-contained, they exist simultaneously with and absorb other media forms. Given the continuous and diverse character of the medium, the viewer always enters televsion in the middle of things.

Correspondingly, the *Flying Circus* episodes begin in medias res, making no reference to any specific moment in time or specific identity of place, as if signaling their ongoing character. The abrupt and arbitrary beginning of each of the programs is further evidence of television as a technological medium that is always on and, unlike film, has no beginning or ending. The loose structure of the shows, their broken-up character, and their movements through different temporal dimensions are characteristic of the flow and heterogeneity of the medium, though many of the episodes make repeated reference to earlier sketches and gestures (e.g., "E. Henry Thripshaw's Disease," "The Spanish Inquisition," and "Njorl's Saga"). The chronological or linear sense of the episodes is scrambled, miming the diversity of the medium. Television's immediacy and liveness is often invoked in the *Flying Circus* through direct address, the play on news reportage, numerous interruptions, and the role of the "Vox Pops" (audience responses that appear spontaneous and introduce "immediate" responses to sketches). Through the appearance of randomness, the *Flying Circus* called attention to the character of television as a "continuous flowing river of experience."[59] This "flowing river" is characterized also by the segmentation of units of time and by "interruption," all of which find their way into the *Flying Circus* addresses of the television medium. The format of the *Flying Circus* reveals that, unlike variety show skits, the episodes have no closure, no culminating punch line, and often seem to have no point.

The uses of animation contributed to the hybrid character of the *Flying Circus* and introduced further disturbances in relation to television time. The viewer was kept constantly off balance not only about the direction, the butt, and the quality of the sketches but also by the disruptive movement from specific places and moments in time to a timeless and phantasmic world. Although Gilliam's animation was connected to the motifs developed in the sketches, it was not mere extension or "support." Rather, the animation functions to highlight the atemporal and hallucinatory character of the *Flying Circus* world. The emphasis on sadistic acts by cartoon figures through images of dismemberment, decapitation, cannibalism, explosions, and various forms of physical mutilation are an invitation to contemplate a world that contradicts altruistic and benign conceptions of behavior.

The fanciful animation, like the appealing images of each of the Pythons, allows entry into a world of unreason where time and space are disordered, as in the case of "The Wacky Queen" sketch that combines photographic cutouts and speeded-up motion as if a silent film has been shown at the wrong speed. In this way, the *Flying Circus* interferes with the recording dimension of television and its anchoring in the present and in real time. For example, "The Wacky Queen" sketch tampers with the historically respectable images of Queen Victoria (Jones) and Prime Minister Gladstone (Chapman). The sketch reminds one of early chase films, thus introducing a version of the past dependent on cinema history. The animation functions in multilayered fashion to juxtapose real time against the creative possibilities of television to alter representation. For example, one colorful, animated episode involves a caterpillar that enters a hut, crawls under a blanket, and emerges as a butterfly. This brief sketch captures the plasticity of television and its capacity to do more than conventional recording or reproduction of stories.

In their cavalier treatment of time, the sketches revealed that television offered the commodity of the packaging and selling of time. In one sketch, "The Time on BBC1," a voice-over (Palin) intones: "Well, its five past nine and nearly time for six past nine. On BBC 2, now it'll shortly be six and a half minutes past nine. Later on this evening it'll be ten o'clock and at 10:30 we'll be joining BBC2 in time for 10:33, and don't forget tomorrow when it'll be 9:20. Those of you who missed 8:45 on Friday will be able to see it again this Friday at a quarter to nine." A second voice-over (Jones) says, "You're a loony," and the first voice-over responds, "I get so bored. I get so bloody bored."

In other sketches involving the BBC, the Pythons call attention to the economic dimensions of television production, emphasizing the relations between television time and monetary value through advertising, sponsorship, and reception, making evident that "the television image is held at a pressure point between innumerable institutions—of regulation, of the market-place, of expressed and inchoate opinion."[60] Such format sketches as "Blackmail," in their ludicrous treatment of the quiz show, underscore connections between time and money as does, more explicitly, the sketch "The BBC Is Short of Money." In "The Money Program," the Presenter (Idle) announces, "Tonight on The Money Program, we're going to look at money. Lots of it. On film and in the studio," and the sketch ends with the song "You can keep your Marxist ways / For it's only just a phase / For it's money, money,

money that makes the world go round."

Television time also involves the labor expended in writing and performing the shows. The Pythons described their working schedule as first taping film inserts, then spending four days in rehearsal, and finally one day filming the show. The least fun was filming, especially when they had to film outside in cold weather; inside filming was preferable, but the most fun, by their own admission, was the writing. The series eschewed canned laughter ("laugh tracks") and opted for live audiences. The Pythons claimed that audiences gave them an indication of reception and thus an opportunity to rethink aspects of the comedy. When they did use canned laughter, it was to call attention to its artificial character.

The Pythons did not always write with the whole group present. They worked most often in pairs and then presented the script to the group for general consideration, at which

"The Wacky Queen"

time they worked out points of disagreement. According to Idle, "We don't work on shows. We tend to go away for a fortnight and write a mass of stuff. Then you come back and meet, everybody reading their material. If it is laughed at, it is put in one pile. If it is not laughed at, we sell it to someone else's show."[61] Idle's tongue-in-cheek description is validated by other members of the group. The only Python who worked largely on his own was Gilliam, because the animation was, for him, a one-person operation. But his animation, reviewed and commented on by the other members of the group, was in the spirit of the sketches and the Python humor. In general, the Pythons had great latitude in creating the series, much more than is characteristic of U.S. television, and the results were consequently a blending of talents through capitalizing on their different strengths and weaknesses.[62]

Along with these other significant dimensions of the relations between time and television, scheduling was a crucial factor in the failure or success of the *Flying Circus*.[63] Whether the failure to provide an advantageous viewing time was due to BBC budgetary constraints or to administrative resistance to the style and substance of the Pythons' work (a form of censorship as mentioned earlier), the show initially suffered in audience ratings. According to critic Stanley Reynolds, "Perhaps, unwittingly, the BBC's failure to give the programme the showing it deserved had something to do with [administrative resistance]."[64] Despite these initial problems, the *Flying Circus* was finally able to find an earlier broadcast time and, subsequently, an audience.

Television Forms and Genres

The comedy of the *Flying Circus* relies on the tropes of explosions and physical mutilation that expand in meaning to include dismemberment of cultural forms. The celebrity interview was among the many television genres that the Pythons dismembered. The television interview would seem to have a major place in the Python world of unreason, and a number of sketches involve a studio setting, with one of the Pythons conducting an interview with an artist, musician, filmmaker, or politician. The sketch initially presents the interviewer as undertaking a serious inquiry of the august personality before reducing the interview encounter to a meaningless exercise in banality, if not aggression. The interviewer's voyeurism comes across through the persistent and personal nature of the questions posed; the interviewee comes across as imprisoned by the conventions of the encounter. Yet the interviewing of famous personalities appears as grotesque as the Gilliam animations interspersed throughout the series. The object, it would seem, not only satirizes this genre but, more profoundly and philosophically, constitutes an attack on existing forms of transmitting information.

The setting of these interviews with "famous figures" takes place in a BBC studio, with the interviewer and subject seated either behind a desk or, more frequently, in armchairs facing each other. The series was not expensive to film, and the limited budget may have been responsible for the inventiveness of the location shots and the spare sets that pass for television studios, bedrooms, cramped living rooms, and offices. In conventional interviews on television, the personalities are questioned by a seemingly dignified interviewer about their lives, the influences on their work, and its "meaning" or "interpretation." An aura of educational seriousness pervades this type of show—except in the hands of the Pythons, where the interview often becomes an exercise in trivialization and humiliation.

In "It's the Arts," a Python interviewer (Cleese) devotes a major part of the interview to establishing an aura of informality by focusing on how to address his guest filmmaker,

"Sir Edward Ross" (Chapman), by name. Cleese asks, "You don't mind if I call you Edward?" Then he shifts to calling him "Ted" and finally "Eddy Baby." The guest gets up angrily, and the interviewer, after using up most of the time, finally turns to the subject and says, "Tell us about your latest film." The film director returns to his seat, accedes to the request to talk, and launches into a lengthy personal history: "Well, the idea came funnily enough when I first joined the industry in 1919," to which the interviewer responds, "Oh, shut up."

In the "Raymond Luxury-Yacht Interview," the interviewer (Palin) sits in the studio across from a man with a polystyrene nose. He introduces him in the conventional mode: "Good evening. I have with me in the studio tonight one of Britain's leading skin specialists—Raymond Luxury-Yacht." The man (Chapman) responds, "That's not my name." Trying again, Palin says, "I'm sorry—Raymond Luxury Yach—t." The man continues: "No, no, no. It's spelled Raymond Luxury-Yach-t, but it's pronounced 'Throatwarbler Mangrove,'" whereupon Palin says, "You're a very silly man, and I'm not going to interview you." The absurdity of the sketch, like so much of the Python comedy, relies on the seemingly nonsensical dialogue, the non sequiturs, the violation of expectations, and the suggestion of the arbitrariness of naming.

The sketch "Arthur 'Two Sheds' Jackson" also focuses on obsession with naming by way of the interview format. Idle, as the interviewer, asks a fictitiously famous musician (Chapman) how he got the name "Two Sheds" and refuses to budge from this subject, even asking his guest if he composed his symphony in the shed. Further destabilizing the interview is the image of a shed behind the two men as the composer vainly seeks to escape the interviewer's insistence on any connection between his name, the image of the shed, and his role as a composer. The progress of the interview is halted because the composer is unable to shift the discussion away from questions about his name. Also, the spontaneity, or rather forced spontaneity, that characterizes such television performances is rendered absurd by the interviewer assuming a condescending and personally intrusive relation to the interviewee, calling attention to his own role and, even more, to the tendency to trivialize dialogue and waste time. The sketch also highlights the complicity of the interviewee in his insistence on claiming his identity via his proper name. The treatment of the interviews with "Sir Edward Ross" and with "Arthur 'Two Sheds'" not only exposes the lack of substantive content in television, particularly in shows that purport to provide information, but also, more fundamentally, reveals the subversive dimensions of Python comedy as residing in the undermining, accepted assumptions about language as a predictable means of communication.

The mission of television to elevate and inform its audiences includes children's programming that involves a "mixture of entertainment, information, and ideas" designed for children of "varying ages, backgrounds, and interests."[65] In the children's programming, learning is often communicated through the persona of the storyteller. In an inversion of this type of program, the *Flying Circus* offers a sketch of a man (Idle) sitting in a cozy armchair and reading a presumably innocuous story in the familiar condescending voice often used to address children on television. However, the anticipated story begins to disintegrate as the narration introduces adult subjects about sexuality and contraception. He tries to return to the children's story and the conventional format of the children's program but is increasingly dismayed by the sexual material that repeatedly disrupts his reading and over which he seems to have no control.

The contrast between the banal and familiar setting and the explosive material that erupts calls attention to television's targeting of specific age groups and the ways in which subjects, especially sexual subjects, are neutralized and contained. Fundamental to most sketches is the exposure of middle-class "authority" and the television medium, which lends the spokespersons the aura of expertise. The viewer has an opportunity to contemplate how television substitutes formulas and clichés for thinking. Through Idle's undermining of the expert's respectability, the viewer also has the opportunity to confront the unseen and unsaid of television. The storyteller's "lapses" in language reiterate a familiar motif in the *Flying Circus*—namely, the role of direct and indirect censorship in programming.

Control of the television apparatus is more explicitly addressed in one of the many "disclaimers" interspersed throughout the *Flying Circus*, an "Apology for Violence and Nudity," in which the voice-over (Idle) announces,

> "The BBC would like to announce that the next scene is not considered suitable for family viewing. It contains scenes of violence, involving people's arms and legs getting chopped off. . . . There are also scenes of naked women with floppy breasts, and also at one point you can see a pair of buttocks, and there's another bit where I'll swear you see everything. . . . Because of the unsuitability of the scene, the BBC will be replacing it with a scene from a repeat of 'Gardening Club' for 1958."

Television is organized, segmented, and diversified in terms of genres structured around codes and conventions familiar to audiences and shaped in their format in order to fit the half-hour or one-hour time slot. However, the BBC was indeed more flexible in its designation of time slots than is characteristic of U.S. commercial networks. The *Flying Circus* was particularly attentive to the array and composition of television genres, presenting through parody and inversion its own versions of melodramas, crime detection, game and quiz shows, news, sports, and historical programs.

The Pythons unsettled the conventional and expected characteristics of genres, refusing narrative closure; stopping a sketch in midstream; interrupting a skit to call attention to the director, the script, or the audience; and especially mixing genres such as situation comedy and melodrama and animation and news.

The sketch "Njorl's Saga," for example, is a mélange of forms, including a historical (Icelandic) epic replete with titles, voice-over narration, and images of the "hero" (Palin) seeking to get on with his "journey," but impeded by the voice-over's lengthy recounting of history and genealogy; contemporary documentary material on industrial development in the town of North Malden that is slipped in by the "North Malden Icelandic Saga Society"; a courtroom drama that involves the transplanted hero who must fight his battles on modern English soil in North Malden; and complaints by a television announcer about the film's "not sticking to the spirit of the original text" and "not ringing true." The announcer is challenged by a man (Chapman) who says, "Quite frankly, I'm sick and tired of people accusing us of being ratings conscious, since popularity is what television is about." The clerk of the court translates this conversation to the judge as "transmitting bland garbage, m'lud."

Still other motifs are interwoven throughout the sketch. For example, the charges against Njorl of "being a foreigner" among other illegal acts are intermingled with a display of police brutality toward him in the person of the arresting officer (Palin). Also folded into this extended sketch are a visit by Mrs. Conclusion (Cleese) and Mrs. Premise (Chapman) to the philosopher Jean Paul Sartre and a segment, "Whicker Island," that is an undoing of the travelogue genre. In the complex interweaving of segments, the casual insertion of credits, the reintroduction of earlier segments, and the mixing of genre forms, the sketch complicates and does violence to expectations of narrative order and unity.

Moreover, any attempt at identifying a unified satiric target of the sketch is undermined. What does remain is an overwhelming sense of television as an unruly and diverse medium complicated by the Pythons' capitilizing on and subversively undermining the ways spectators are habituated to this diversity.

The Pythons' transgressive treatment of television involves a reflexive focus about visibility and invisibility: what people see, what eludes their gaze through habituation, and what might be seen differently. A comic technique employed by the *Flying Circus* to upset accustomed viewing responses is the previously mentioned format sketch. Predictable styles of television representation are de-familiarized by being "emptied" and replaced "with something ludicrous,"[66] as in the sketch "The Attila the Hun Show," featuring Cleese, Palin, Chapman, Idle, and Cleveland. The linking of recognizable stock film footage (drawn from not one but several archival sources) to situation comedy produces a jarring effect. Both the "epic" cinematography and the sitcom are emptied of their familiar contexts through association with each other and made to appear ludicrous. However, the sketch—through the characters' names, the image of a decapitated bloody head (looking very like Terry Gilliam's), and Attila's line, "I want you kids to get a-head"—injects the alien subject of violence into the sitcom. The use of canned laughter further underscores the parodic elements in and the staginess of the sketch.

The sketch begins with an image of Huns on horseback, accompanied by conventional voice-over providing a pompous commentary on "the once mighty Roman Empire . . . exposed to the Barbarian hordes to the east." However, this mock epic is transformed quickly into a domestic situation comedy set in an American-style living room, with Attila returning home after a day's work:

Attila (Cleese): Oh, darling I'm home.

Mrs. Attila (Cleveland): Hello darling. Had a busy day at the office?

Attila: Not at all bad. (Playing to camera) Another merciless sweep across Central Europe.

(Canned laughter)

Mrs. Attila: I won't say I'm glad to see you, but boy, am I glad to see you.

(Enormous canned laughter and applause. Enter two kids.)

Jenny (Chapman): Hi, daddy.

Robin (Palin): Hi, daddy.

Attila: Hi Jenny, hi Robby. (Brief canned applause) Hey, I've got a present for you two kids in that bag. (They pull out a severed head.) I want you kids to get a-head.

The sketch includes a blackfaced "Rochester" (Idle), named Uncle Tom, who serves Attila a drink. Then after more stock images of Huns on horseback, the sketch breaks off with an announcer declaring, "And now for something completely different." "The Attila the Hun Show" draws on the colloquial character and clichéd language of sitcoms. The invocation of decapitation, castration, uncontrolled aggression, and violence, and the yoking of these elements with the sanitized world of sitcoms derails conventional responses and renders the familiar world grotesque. Later in the program, the subject of Attila is reintroduced in "The Attila the Bun" sketch by means of animation showing images of a vicious rampaging bun, whereby even more transgressive aspects of Python humor are unleashed. The carnivalesque is not gentle, and Python humor is manifest not only in Gilliam's animated images but also in the tendency of the *Flying Circus* to undermine narrative continuity in the endless and anarchic play of language, the dizzying pace of the images, and the multiple associations spectators are invited to entertain.

The sketches are intertextual, drawing on particular moments of British television. They also depend on allusions to existing American programs, especially game shows, and their British appropriations. One of the most frequent roles played by Palin is that of an American-style announcer, often dressed in loud red or plaid jackets in contrast to conservative BBC announcers. Palin speaks with constantly rising tonal inflection and describes events in language larded with hyperbole. At the same time, he hops frenetically from place to place. On one occasion, he is host to a variety show that features an act, "Arthur Ewing and His Musical Mice," where mice are bludgeoned to death. The "organ" consists of rows of mice, and the "music" is of the mice's last squeal as the "musician" (Jones), weilding a mallet, smashes them. In this sketch, as in others in which Palin is a quiz show host, the focus is on the exploitative, violent, and sadistic content and style of television programs that are conventionally masked or made to appear playful and benevolent.

Similarly, the "authoritative" art critic, played by Idle, interprets significant films to the television audience. As Philip Jenkinson, Idle discusses a cinematic genre known as the "Cheese Western" (e.g., "Gunfight at Gruyère Corral") as a cross between Truman Capote and "a pederast vole." Idle's introduction is a prelude to a screening of the films of one of the host's "favorite directors," the American Sam Peckinpah, most notorious for the violence of such films as *The Wild Bunch* (1969) and *Straw Dogs* (1971). The film selected by Jenkinson, "Salad Days," begins innocuously; the script for the sketch describes "a lyrical scene of boys in white flannels and girls in pretty dresses frolicking on a lawn to the accompaniment of a piano played by one of the boys."

After conventional shots of the group, accompanied by

banal dialogue, the sketch dissolves into a violent spectacle as body parts are severed and blood flows freely. The "film clip" clashes with the "critic's" bland and sycophantic television discussion of the film, while the violent images remain unacknowledged by the verbal commentary. In this sketch, the Pythons provide a reflexive, critical commentary on Peckinpah's treatment of violence and on their own work. Eschewing direct moralizing, the Pythons acknowledge the brutality of Peckinpah's scenarios, but at the same time they share with their viewers (as they do in so many of their other skits and akin to Peckinpah's films) images of a world that not only thrives on mutilation, blood, and violent death but seems intent on making these images of violence palatable. Furthermore, the transgressive dimension of the sketch resides in its explosion of the orderly and idyllic world through the unexplained, unanticipated, and relentless disembodiment of the figures.

The game show is not exempt from the Python televi-

Getting "A-Head" in "The Attila the Hun Show"

sion encyclopedia. In "Blackmail," with Palin as the flashy host, an individual is threatened with portions of film flashed on a screen that show him or her in a compromising situation. The host calls the guilty parties and threatens to show more of the film to the television audience unless the blackmail money is paid: "Yes, Mrs. Teal, if you'll send us fifteen pounds sterling we'll never reveal the rest of this picture." In the case of a recalcitrant "contestant," the host runs a money meter, raising the price until the contestant calls in and tells the host to stop the film. This skit is not a gentle "spoof" on television game shows: it is a biting and not terribly funny dissection of such shows. The strategy employed in this sketch is consistent with the Pythons' forms of comedy in the blatantly familiar carnivalesque strategy of turning the world upside down. The sketch, emphasizing the cruel and sadistic aspects of behavior in ways consistent with Gilliam's cartoons, declares war on sentiment through underlining acquisitive and hostile aspects of behavior often taken for granted in seemingly inoffensive television programs.

Numerous sketches in the *Flying Circus* that focus on violence are a reminder of television as a purveyor of catastrophe. For example, images of physical violence are repeated regularly in the animated opening segments of each episode in the series. Gilliam's repeated emphasis on cannibalism, violence, murder, and dismemberment runs parallel to sketches such as "The Piranha Brothers" (an allusion to the notorious Kray brothers?) and "The Dull Life of a City Stockbroker." In each of these, the Pythons complicate the images of mutilation and explosions by focusing not only on the venality of the perpetrators but also on the complicity of the victims. For example, one of the Piranha victims, Stig O'Tracy (Idle), when confronted by an interviewer who asks, "I've been told Dinsdale Piranha nailed your head to the floor," responds, "No. Never. He was a smashing bloke. He used to buy his mother flowers and that. He was like a brother to me." When confronted by evidence that this event was filmed, Stig says, "Oh yeah, he did that. . . . Well, he had to, didn't he? I mean, there was nothing else he could do, be fair. I had transgressed the unwritten law."

The world of the "dull stockbroker" is an instance of an "escalation sketch" described by Roger Wilmut in his book *From Fringe to Flying Circus*. The sketch, characteristic of Python humor, is composed of escalating incidents of violence against others—bludgeoning, shootings, hijacking, and explosions—to which the stockbroker (Palin) is completely oblivious. Despite the confusion that surrounds him, the stockbroker miraculously escapes, and when he reaches the office, he picks up a luridly violent magazine. This sketch introduces yet another aspect of the Python treatment of violence evident in "Salad Days" and "Attila the Hun," among many other sketches. Acts of violence are combined with a reflexive focus on visibility and invisibility: what people see

"Salad Days": A Sam Peckinpah "Picnic"

and what eludes their gaze through normalization. For example, although the stockbroker is unable to see the violence that surrounds him, he can look at it when it is reproduced in print.

Similarly, in "People Falling from Buildings," a man (Idle), observing bodies flying through the air, alerts his indifferent coworker (Cleese) to the sight. Without visible affect, the men disagree and make a bet about the identity of the victims. Both of these sketches involve images of violence tied to the moral dilemma of indifference to viewing violence. The *Flying Circus* invokes the ubiquity of violence that pervades television: gruesome images of the world are selectively and repeatedly aired on television and assumed to be "normal." Through a diminution of affect and incongruous juxtaposition, the Pythons render obvious the habituated responses to violence conveyed by television.

A major source of information about the contemporary world is derived from television news programming, with its data involving local, regional, national, and international

A Python-Style Game Show

events. Not surprisingly, many of the sketches tamper with forms of news reportage. The Python "reports" can involve a news story of Pablo Picasso doing a painting as he rides a bicycle or a stock market report on the rising or falling value of body parts or an episode reporting the filming of "Scott of the Antarctic" and "Scott of the Sahara." Often the news is interrupted as the commentator shifts from one site to another, clearly struggling to fill those moments with banal dialogue when nothing is happening in the main story. The news is delivered by a newsreader situated behind a desk in an enclosed studio with a prepared script, reporting on the events of the day in sober tones. But what would happen if he were forcibly removed from his customary position?

The Pythons contemplate this possibility in the sketch "Stolen Newsreader." The absurdity of the sketch relies on the drama of stealing a newsreader—not money or jewels. His report ranges from information concerning trade in Poland, Russia, and the United Kingdom; death; Mr. Charles Griffith's loss of his National Savings book; the results of a cricket match; and weather prediction. This list of disconnected, uninformative, and incongruous sound bytes is communicated in impeccable English. By forcibly removing the newsreader from the studio, the sketch dislodges him from his familiar position, but the "something different" of the comedy resides in its radical solution to the routine television scenario of reporting. The sketch does not merely ridicule the absurdity of news coverage; it aggressively poses a "solution"—getting rid of this nuisance by dramatically dumping the newsreader into the river. The humor of the sketch depends on its creating an extreme situation to unsettle customary forms of seeing that we may recognize but to which we give little thought.

The "Stolen Newsreader," played by Cleese, is kidnapped from the television studio while he is on the air. As his desk is placed on a truck and carried through the city, he conducts his news reporting without interruption and without the slightest acknowledgement of his situation, indifferent to the fact that his own kidnapping is news. Also evident is the indifference of spectators who observe the incongruity of his reporting while being kidnapped. By removing the newsreader from the studio, the sketch dislodges him from his "normal" positioning behind a desk. His continuing to read the news heightens to absurdity the sense in which he is wedded to his script. The climax of dumping Cleese in the river provides a humorous "solution" to the banality if not irrelevance and ineffectuality of much news reporting.

In another reflexive sketch focusing on a newsreader, Idle, sitting in the newsroom at his desk, reports on a jewel theft. The apparel of the thief he describes resembles his own clothing, and the image on the monitor behind him shows him being taken away for interrogation about the robbery by a constable. Idle then reports that the man has been released. Later, he announces that the police have focused their search on a newsreader in the London area, and now Idle is removed from his desk as his image in the rear monitor continues reporting. Doubling, through the use of the two TV images, the "live" one and the one on the monitor, raises not only the issue of the character of "liveness" of television but also the question of which image is "real."

The *Flying Circus* also entertains the drama of sports reporting on television—but with a difference. One sketch mixes sports with art, reporting on the progress of Pablo Picasso who is painting while riding a bicycle. As the reporter waits on the road for Picasso to appear, he provides descriptions of others on bikes, including their spills, and generally filling the time with anything that comes to mind. Combining Picasso with bicycling is only one aspect of the incongruous situation: the dialogue exposes the banality of the reportage. The sketch becomes another instance of spending time on nonevents that involve personalities assumed to be of significance to the viewer. Other Python sketches involving sports events—cricket, soccer, and tennis matches—and daredevil feats as reported on television end in anticlimax. For example, one sketch focuses on sports reporters in a studio sitting behind a desk surrounded by numerous bottles of liquor they consume frenetically. While television sports reporting maximizes the excitement of sports events, the behind-the-scenes portrait of the inebriated commentators reduces and subverts the dramatic flourishes associated with this type of reporting.

Even the sports documentary is not exempt from dismemberment. The "Mosquito Hunters" focuses on the virile sport of hunting animals. The huntsmen, Hank (Chapman) and Roy (Idle), embark on their day's adventure. The voice-over (Cleese) announces, "Hank and Roy Spire are tough, fearless backwoodsmen who have chosen to live in the violent, unrelenting world of nature's creatures, where only the

The "Stolen Newsreader"

fittest survive. Today they are off to hunt mosquitoes." The sketch relies on understatement and incongruity to expose the inflated language of masculinity characteristic of the televisual sports world. The contrast between the ammunition the men carry and their object—destroying tiny creatures—is reinforced by conventional images of hunters and the pompous voice-over that "reports" the conquests. The voice-over stresses the warlike "preparedness" of the hunters while the visuals stress the minuscule insects that they kill. The sketch ends with an image of the two men standing by an armored vehicle as the voice-over intones, "Wherever there is a challenge, Hank and Roy Spire will be there ready to carry on this primordial struggle between man and inoffensive, tiny insects."

Consistently, television genres get confused with each other—historical dramas, game shows, and melodramas. Wolfgang Amadeus Mozart, as played by Cleese, sitting at a piano, hosts a program that numerically tallies famous deaths. Dressed in eighteenth-century garb, Cleese announces, "Hello again, and welcome to the show. Tonight we continue to look at some famous deaths. Tonight we start with the wonderful death of Genghis Khan. Take it away, Genghis." When the scorecards are held up, it appears that St. Stephen has won the contest as the most "famous death," and Mozart expresses his condolences to Genghis Khan. He also blandly announces the "week's request death," ending the program with "Oh blimey, how time flies. Sadly we are reaching the end of another programme and so it's finale time." But the bizarre sketch is not over. Admiral Nelson now plunges to his death shouting, "Kiss me, Hardy!"

A similar disturbance of expectations about television genres is characteristic of the "The Spanish Inquisition" sketch, which combines drawing-room comedy, historical drama, and commentary by a BBC announcer on jokes and punch lines. The sketch begins in a predictable upper-class drawing room, but the moment that one of the characters introduces the word inquisition, the scenario moves into another register by disrupting the formulas associated with drawing-room and historical drama. Suddenly three cardinals, played by Palin, Jones, and Gilliam dressed in brilliant red robes, appear, and the viewer is treated to dialogue that evokes the cruelty of the Inquisition. The cardinals stumble over their lines as they try to describe the "chief weapons of the Inquisition": "fear, surprise, ruthless efficiency, an almost fanatical devotion to the Pope, and nice red uniforms."

The "Inquisitioners" are brought into being by the mere articulation of the word *inquisition*. The Pythons' inability to remember their lines forces them out of "character" and interrupts the flow of the sketch. They have to leave several times to begin again. The "Inquisitioners" are constantly sidetracked in their banter with each other and with their

"The Spanish Inquisition"

"victims" and in their recollections of their status and roles. In seeking to "torture" their victims, they are unable to find the requisite instruments for torture; hence they improvise a dish rack as a substitute for the "rack." After the "digressions" of a BBC announcer and an insert of a political interview on taxation, the sketch is returned to when the "Inquisitioners" reappear and "torture" an elderly woman by forcing her to sit in a "comfy" armchair so that she will "confess" to "heresy." The "Inquisitioners" are arbitrarily reintroduced in a later courtroom scene. In none of their appearances is there any pretense of continuity, closure, or even a logical set of connections between the "Inquisitioners," their "victims," the BBC announcer, and the discussion in a Civil Service committee room on taxation.

Like other Python sketches, "The Spanish Inquisition" is the quintessence of the non sequitur. The relation to a brutal moment of the historical past is called forth through the word *inquisition*, but the sketch finally has very little to do with explaining or dramatizing that earlier epoch. The treatment of words and images produces a form of illogic that is carnivalesque, undermining any expectation of narrative coherence or conventional strategies for engaging with knowledge and belief. In short, commonsense becomes nonsense.

Animals, Insects, Machines, and Human Bodies

In keeping with the propensity of Python comedy to focus on the physical body, and particularly on cultural taboos and restraints on language and behavior, many of the Python sketches involve images of and allusions to nudity, sexual practices, and forms of censorship. The *Flying Circus* once again invokes television as a conduit to unsettle habituated forms of response to gesture and thinking. The comic images the Pythons adopt in the forms of the sketches and in the animation rely on magical thinking. As in Ovid's *Metamorphosis*, and in all kinds of fantasy and satire, animals are endowed with human attributes. For example, dogs turn out to be U.S. secret agents, as in the "Mr. Neutron" sketches. The Python world is saturated with unpredictable transformations—from animal to human, from realist style to fantasy, from photograph to animation, from sense to nonsense, and from cool delivery to hysterical and inappropriate rant. Inanimate objects become animate. These metamorphoses ridicule the cultural restraints placed on the human body and on all forms of language, both gestural and verbal. They also undermine assumptions about human uniqueness and rationality.

Animals change their attributes, adopting each other's characteristics. "Flying Sheep" is based on overturning the identity of sheep as timid creatures and ascribing aggressive and violent behavior to them. The viewer does not see these "menaces" but is privy to their behavior through the dialogue of two men, one a city man, the other a farmer. Or, in the sketch "Killer Sheep," a husband, Mr. Concrete (Jones) and his wife (Palin) discover that a rodent in the wainscoting turns out to be a sheep with a gun. The rat catcher (Chapman) informs the couple that "normally a sheep is a placid, timid creature, but you've got a killer."

One of the abiding comical figures in the Python gallery of instruction is the lecturer "qualified" to speak on any topic—animals, plants, movies, art, and philosophy—but always from an eccentric position. Lectures are reinforced by "slides" that provide no direct information on the subject but are distracting, calling attention to a disjunction between words and images. Not only does the human body become the subject of investigation, often through animation, but also the body is invoked through the association with animals, frequently sheep. For example, the "French Lecture on Sheepcraft" presents Cleese and Palin in striped T-shirts and berets, giving a lecture with a "visual aid"—an image of sheep that has sliding segments for different parts of the body, including what the Pythons refer to in other contexts as "naughty bits."

In this sketch, the naughtiness is subverted through the conflation of animals, machines, and the (implied) human body verbally masked through the use of the French language. The complexity of this episode entails connections between the animal and the machine, because the sheep's internals, it turns out, are the inside of an aircraft. This sketch is another instance in which Python carnivalesque humor is engaged in a continuous blurring and hence subverting of distinctions between humans and animals, animals and machines, and mind and body. The focus is once again on those parts of the body barred from discourse. The "lecturers" move from front to back of their specimen, making sure that "the naughty bits" of the sheep are not lost on the viewer. Nor is the cultural restraint on directly naming

parts of the body: the use of a "foreign" language is another instance of how the Pythons subvert the role of censorship.

In one of the interview sketches, "The Man with Three Buttocks," the interviewer (Cleese), with slides behind him, has difficulty finding a "respectable" word with which to conduct the interview with his subject. He tries *rump*, *posterior*, and *derrière* before he can spit out the word "buttock." But the critical moment in the sketch occurs with the appearance of a television camera. According to the interviewer, the camera is brought in to enable the television viewer a "quick visual" of the offending part, but the "man with three buttocks" resists this attempt. Not only does the sketch continue the Python-esque preoccupation with "naughty bits" of the body that are excised from conventional television practice, but it also persists in the tendency of the medium to arouse, but not realize, expectations of viewing "naughty bits." The sketches concerning bodily parts are interwoven throughout the series, particularly exemplified in the sketch "How to Recognize Different Parts of the Body" and in the many animated sequences that focus on nudity, dismemberment, decapitation, disembodied but moving teeth, a huge foot crushing everything beneath it, and humans metamorphosed into animals.

The sketches involving animals are also woven into news reporting. In the "News for Parrots," an animated image of a parrot precedes the narrator's (Palin) delivery of the events of the day. "Good evening. Here is the news for parrots. No parrots were involved in an accident on M1 today, when a lorry carrying high-octane fuel was in collision with a hollard . . . that is a bollard and not a parrot. A spokesman said he was glad no parrots were involved." The narrator also announces a version of *A Tale of Two Cities* adapted for parrots, but has no news to report of gibbons, because they were not "involved today in an accident on the M1."

While discussions of visual style are commonly reserved for descriptions of cinema, the style of the *Flying Circus*, for all of its emphasis on verbal humor—pun, innuendo, double entendre—is cinematic in its treatment of the body. The impetus toward comedy, as the Pythons acknowledged, came from such silent cinema figures as Charlie Chaplin and Buster Keaton, whose comedy relied heavily on facial and physical gestures. In the *Flying Circus*, even when the focus is on the stationary character of conventional "talk" television, the Pythons' strategy of calling attention to its static qualities is through the introduction of gesture—contrasting background images, facial grimaces, body movement, and repetition of familiar, but in this context inappropriate, gesticulation. For example, "Cleese has spent much of his career playing with devastating effect seething, angry, mentally volcanic characters who if pushed just one more inch will erupt in a ranting, fist-shaking, quavering rage—and

The French Lecture on Sheepcraft

then, of course, are pushed that one inch . . . stomping his feet, beating his head against walls, smacking menials or dashing around in a state of semi-hysteria."[67] One of the most famous of the Python gestures is the "silly walk," associated with Cleese as "The Minister of Silly Walks." The choreographed and exaggerated movements ridicule the conformity that trickles down from the various government ministries, producing a generation of silly walkers. But the "silly walk" also visualizes the Python concern with the captive body. The "silly walk" emphasizes the rigidity of the back, the spastic character of each leg, one raised after the other, reminiscent of Tourette's syndrome and suggestive of a loss of freedom of movement. The deserved popularity of this sketch relies in part on its spoofing of bureaucracy, but, more fundamentally, it evokes a world of madness through gestures that are similar to photos of patients in mental hospitals and indicative of the discipline and control of the gesture. The "silly walk" exaggerates the body's imprisonment in gesture.

The dead or dying body is not exempt from the Pythons' preoccupation with physicality, calling attention to the claims of the body and to mortality, a subject usually treated in melodramatic or tragic fashion. The dead speak in some of the sketches, and corpses and undertakers play significant roles in the Python cosmos. One of the sketches begins with six undertakers carrying a coffin. Each drops dead while carrying the coffin so that none is left alive when the coffin finally reaches the cemetery. This sketch was subject to BBC criticism, but not eliminated, nor was a later sketch involving a corpse who is brought to a courtroom as a witness: the defense attorney insists that the dead man can "speak" from his coffin. Likewise, a later animation sketch featuring a prince who discovers a cancerous "Black Blot" also drew criticism. After objections on the part of BBC authorities, the "cancer" was changed to "gangrene."

One of the courtroom sketches (a familiar setting for British humor, melodrama, and satire on film and television) focuses on a witness at a murder trial—a corpse who "speaks" by tapping the coffin in response to Inspector Dim of the Yard's questions. In the spirit of film and television crime genres, the scenario seems conventional enough, but the Pythons' treatment relies on a more fundamental engagement with death that entails the treatment of the corpse and of death in unsentimental fashion without euphemism. For example, in an encounter between a funeral director and a man who wants to solve the problem of what to do with his mother's dead body, the director tells the man that he has three choices: bury the body, burn it, or, in keeping with the Python mastery of the shock effect, "eat it." Once again, this sketch underscores the Python penchant for blurring all boundaries, including those between life and death that are conventionally sealed off from each other and treated piously.

Featuring "therapy" for animals is another strategy of the *Flying Circus*' corruption of boundaries, in this instance,

Python Undertakers

between human and animal. Sketches involve killer sheep, depressed cats, and mice that turn out to be sheep. In one sketch, a husband and wife, Mr. A and Mrs. B, are troubled by their cat's depressed behavior and call in a "Confuse-A-Cat" team to animate their ailing cat. The animal "therapists" perform a series of sketches to entertain the cat and to alleviate its "symptoms" of "catatonia." The veterinarian, utilizing psychiatric language, informs the couple, "Your cat is suffering from what we Vets haven't found a word for." His condition is typified "by total physical inertia, absence of interest in its ambience—what we Vets call environment—failure to respond to the conventional external stimuli—a ball of string, a nice juicy mouse, a bird. To be blunt, your cat is in a rut." The cat is not moved by the performances and finally retreats to the house in exasperation or greater depression.

Other sketches invoke therapy for psychic malaise, involving marriage counseling, fake psychiatrists, and demented Gumby psychiatrists and their Gumby patients.

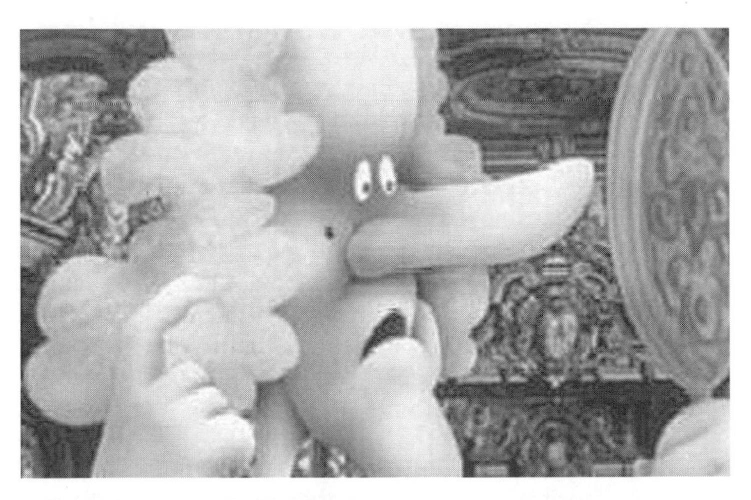

"What's in a Name": "The Black Blot"

Even bad acting can be treated. The hospital ward for bad actors, especially Shakespearian actors, highlights the pervasive and intrusive role of popular psychotherapy, the Pythons' fascination with madness, and connections between madness and performance. Psychology assumes a key role in the "topsy-turvy" world inhabited by the Python characters; it functions not as an explanation or mitigation for psychic "problems" but as an index of the disjunction between the categories of normality and pathology. The "pathological" is normal in the world of the Pythons, where folly prevails. What critics have described as the surrealism of the sketches and animation is derived from the inversion of sanity and madness at the heart of the series. The "characters"—human and other animals—expose the lack of reason and constraint, and their "maladies," as such, are not subject to "melioration." Python humor relies on the infringement of boundaries between the normal and the pathological, and the Pythons confront and shock their viewers through their violation of accepted limits of expression.

Cross-Dressing and Gender Bending

In the context of British comedy, drag is not unusual, but in the 1960s and 1970s, during what has come to be known as the "sexual revolution," the use of cross-dressing took on a spectacularly subversive cultural dimension. This "revolution" became identified with critiques of male and female roles, emerging gay critiques, and a general tendency to blur familiar sexual, class, and gendered boundaries of heterosexual dominance. The *Flying Circus* introduced terms that named and directly addressed homophobic language and behavior: references to "poofs" and the fear of being a "poof" are liberally sprinkled throughout sketches.

In the tradition of university revues, cross-dressing was hardly extraordinary. Nor was cross-dressing alien to British film comedy. Old Mother Riley, an old Irish washerwoman, played by Arthur Lucan, was popular in the cinema of the 1940s, and occasionally the *Carry On* series featured men in drag (e.g., *Carry On Nurse*, 1959). In the *Flying Circus*, women were for the most part played by men. Female actors were imported to take part in certain sketches. In the series, "real" women play conventional femme roles for the most part. Cleveland played femme fatales, upper-class wives, and secretaries. She was cast in sexy parts: erring wives with a roving eye, fashion models, buxom nurses and receptionists, television game show hostesses, or female accomplices or victims in crime detection skits. On a few occasions, she assumed a male role. For example, in a courtroom sketch, "Multiple Murderers," she played a male juror in the trial of a repentant murderer, played melodramatically by Idle, who convinces the jury of his guilt to the point that they forgive his crimes. Gender reversal in the *Flying Circus* is parallel to the series' consistent practice of inverting all roles involving social class and national and generational identities.

An instance of "cruising" involves a brief sketch of a man who encounters a police officer and wants to be "arrested" for a criminal infraction. However, it turns out that that man is seeking a sexual encounter, and the two saunter off together. Then there are skits that invert heterosexual practices, such as the "Scotsman on a Horse" who appears to be rescuing his ladylove from marriage. He rides to the church, disrupts the ceremony, and carries off the groom, not the bride.

One sketch, "Nudge Nudge," often singled out for comment and praise by reviewers and fans highlights an encounter between two men in a bar played by Idle and Jones. Idle as "Norman" confronts Jones, referred to in the script as "Him," with overly familiar questions. For example, Norman asks, "Is your wife a go-er? Know what I mean.

Your wife, does she, er, does she 'go'—eh? eh? eh? Know what I mean, Know what I mean, Nudge nudge, Nudge nudge. Know what I mean? Say no more. . . . Know what I mean?" At one point, in response to Norman's question about Jones's wife's interest in "candid photography," Jones responds, "Look, are you insinuating something?" Idle's smarmy familiarity is conveyed in the way he repeats everything twice: "Nudge, nudge," "Say no more, Say no more," "I bet she does, I bet she does," "wink, wink," and "grin, grin." The sketch captures the character of the bore, his invasion of another's privacy, his voyeurism, and the language and gesture characteristic of casual social encounters.

The *Flying Circus* unsentimentally inverted, exposed, and exploded institutionalized representations of gender and sexuality expressed and disseminated broadly through the culture and through media. One of the most oft-cited sketches from the *Flying Circus* for its inversion of predictable gendered and sexual representation is "The Lumberjack Song," in which Palin, with Cleveland at his side, and a chorus of men dressed as Canadian Mounties, sing what seems to be an innocuous song in praise of the virility of lumberjacking. Reversing associations with the Mounties in popular literature and film, the episode "tarnishes" familiar images of masculinity by invoking and transgressing the cultural animus toward masculine appropriation of feminine behavior. The Mountie, played by Palin, is the barber of a previous episode who struggles against his murderous inclinations. This violence is then appended to his wayward image as a discontented male. In keeping with the Pythons' steady erosion of dominant forms of sexuality, the song extends beyond the familiar cross-dressing associated with comedy to amplify and undermine the dimensions of gendered and sexual behavior usually ignored, caricatured, or soft-pedaled in the commercial world of mass media. Rather than relying on action and spoken dialogue, the sketch is a musical interlude, relying on the disjunction between the lilting quality of the musical sounds and the jarring lyrics.

Drag is a major Python strategy to reverse viewer expectations about traditional social, and particularly professional, roles. In the sketch "Poofy Judges," Idle and Palin disrobe after leaving the courtroom. Underneath their judge's robes they are dressed in feminine attire. Moreover, their conversation about the courtroom is, in the vein of stereotypical feminine gossip, replete with hand flourishes. In "Face the Press," featuring an interview with the "Minister of Home Affairs" (Chapman), the moderator (Idle) describes the minister's attire as if the news program were a fashion show, describing his "striking organza dress in pink tulle, with matching pearls and a diamante collar necklace," shoes "in brushed pigskin," and hair done "by Roger." When asked a question about his political position, the minister responds, "I'd like to answer the question in two ways. First in my normal speaking voice, and then in a kind of silly, high-pitched whine." The feminizing of the minister ridicules the pretentiousness and vacuity of political roles, the type of television show that lends itself to the gossip format, and, as always in the *Flying Circus*, the ambiguous and tenuous character of femininity.

In a domestic sketch featuring the Pythons in drag, two housewives, Mrs. Conclusion (Chapman) and Mrs. Premise (Cleese), seated in a Laundromat, discuss the "burying of a cat" and the "putting down of a budgie." After examining the pros and cons of extermination, the sketch ends with the possibility of flushing creatures "down the loo," but Mrs. Conclusion says, "No, you shouldn't do that. . . . They 'breed' in the sewers." But then the sketch takes a more culturally "elevated" turn as Mrs. Conclusion introduces the seeming non sequitur, "It's a funny thing, freedom. I mean, how can any of us be really free when we still have personal possessions?" Mrs. Premise answers, "You can't. You can't. I mean, how can I go off and join Frelimo when I've got nine installments to pay on the fridge?" And Mrs. Conclusion responds, "No, you can't. You can't. Well this is the whole crux of Jean Paul Sartre's *Roads to Freedom*." Because Mrs. Premise had met Sartre's wife once "on holiday," the "women" decide to take a trip to Paris to get an answer to whether Sartre's masterpiece "is an allegory of man's search for commitment." The sketch breaks off with Mrs. Premise calling Mrs. Sartre on the telephone in broken French.

Later in the same show, still dressed in their house frocks, the two find themselves before an apartment house with its directory of famous occupants—including the Duke and Duchess of Windsor, Jean Genet and friend, and Indira Gandhi—and they ring a bell. "Mrs. Sartre" is running a vacuum cleaner in the apartment when the "women" are admitted and told they can have a brief audience with the great man (himself under the influence of six glasses of wine) to ask him the question that has brought them to Paris. Sartre's

"I Wish I'd Been a Girlie"

voice is heard off camera as he answers their question about whether his book *Roads to Freedom* is an allegory of "man's search for commitment" with a brief "oui."

Cross-dressing prevails in another skit with two "housewives" who bring their children to an art museum, where the children destroy the paintings. The conversation of the women alternates between pretentious, inflated comments on the paintings and ineffectual reprimands to the children, who are tearing and even eating the artwork. These sketches and many others, including two portraying Beethoven's and Mozart's domestic lives (again with the Pythons playing their wives), employ cross-dressing to unsettle prevailing conceptions of dominant heterosexual domestic life. The domestic milieu is cramped and spare. The "women" are dowdy. The sketches invert commonplace conceptions about the relationship between quotidian life and high culture. In the case of Mrs. Premise and Mrs. Conclusion, Sartre's existential philosophy is situated in the pragmatic dimensions of daily existence, and Beethoven's and Mozart's

The "Poofy Judges"

domestic lives appear to be mundane, even sordid. "The New Cooker Sketch" features Jones as Mrs. Pinnet, who encounters difficulties with the delivery, receipt, and connection of a stove. Ultimately, she learns that she can best get immediate service through being gassed by the deliverymen. The domestic sketches capture the difficulties of everyday life involved in housecleaning, minding children, or in getting new appliances, but through the added dimension of drag and through grotesque forms of inversion and exaggeration (the eating of paintings and the gassing of a customer), the *Flying Circus* turns quotidian life upside down.

Housewives are often associated with television viewing. The "Pepperpots" (named in the scripts but not in the shows and played by the Pythons) comment on advertisements and on televised events. Interspersed throughout the *Flying Circus* and captured in on-the-street interviews by an announcer, the use of the Pepperpots captures the tendency of television to focus on

Mrs. Premise and Mrs. Conclusion

"live" encounters with viewers. The Pepperpots offer opinions on the particular advertised products or viewpoints on contemporary events. A counterpart to the Pepperpots is also evident in the many sketches (such as "The Death of Mary, Queen of Scots" and "Exploding Penguin on a TV Set") that involve two women (also Pythons in drag) sitting before a TV and watching particular shows. The emphasis on connections between housewives, advertising, and the medium of television also introduces the issue of spectatorship and the home as site of reception. In this fashion, too, the Pythons further emphasize the domestic and domesticating character of television.

In addition to harassed housewives, overworked mothers, and women on the street who are hip to advertising, there are the enormous and threatening women in animated sequences and the historical figures such as Queen Victoria who are treated irreverently as, for example, in the "Wacky Queen," where the Queen hoses Gladstone and chases him

The Pepperpots

around a garden. There are also several irreverent portraits of Princess Margaret. Age also plays a prominent role in the *Flying Circus*. In the skit "Hell's Grannies," old women stand in for motorcycle gangs such as "Hell's Angels," offering a shocking reversal from usual expectations via stereotypes of older women. The sketch opens with the voice of a reporter announcing, "This is a frightened city. Over these houses, over these streets hangs a pall of fear. Fear of a new kind of violence which is terrorizing the city. Yes, gangs of old ladies attacking defenseless, fit young men."

The "Hell's Grannies" are portrayed wearing long black dresses trimmed with white lace at the neck and on the sleeves, small black hats trimmed with flowers, and carrying black handbags over their arms, though on their motorcycles they are clothed in black leather jackets. The announcer describes the "grannies" as "old hoodlums," "layabouts in lace," and "senile delinquents." These "old ladies" are remi-

"Hell's Grannies"

niscent of one of Ealing's last comedies, *The Ladykillers* (1955), where a little old lady, Mrs. Wilberforce, outwits the crooks who have come to stay in her house and commit a bank robbery, from which she ultimately profits. In the Python skit, the "old ladies" are no longer sedate, eccentric old people but hip to the demands of the new violence and are able to outwit the police.

The Pythons' caricatures of femininity, heterosexuality, and homosexuality are not congenial to supporters of identity politics: they do not present "desirable" and affirmative gendered images to emulate. Unflinchingly, the *Flying Circus* unsentimentally offers inverted, exposed, and exploded institutionalized representations of gender and sexuality as they are expressed and disseminated broadly through the culture and through the medium of television.

Hyperbole, Excess, and Escalation

Melodrama is excessive, relying on décor as well as verbal and visual cues to communicate a superfluity of affect, escalation, and overstatement of wrongs perpetrated against innocent victims. The *Flying Circus* self-consciously employs these excessive strategies of melodrama as a striking means of estranging and confusing the viewer about events. The tactic of starting with what appears to be a trivial incident and then inflating it is characteristic of many of the sketches and of Gilliam's animation. The sketches begin with an incident that seems innocent enough—a job interview, problems with a pet (e.g., "Confuse-a-Cat"), a mundane incident in a Laundromat, a family reunion—and then escalate into hyperbole and excess.

Many skits involve two persons, one behind a desk and one in front of the desk in the seat of a petitioner, whether an applicant for a job, a consumer lodging a complaint about a purchase, a criminal violator interrogated by police or customs officials, a needy person seeking help from a psychiatrist or counselor, or a person seeking to settle an insurance claim. In all cases, these encounters (often with Cleese behind the desk and Palin as the petitioner or subject of investigation) are characterized by the official's incapacity to hear properly, his nugatory attitude toward any question or request, and his refusal to accede to a simple request, constantly shifting the ground of the interaction. The petitioner is usually naïve and therefore highly suggestible and malleable. In all cases, the sketches employ the same tactic of escalating the affect in the form of growing impatience and desperation until one or the other of the characters (usually the petitioner) is forced to capitulate. Excess resides in the disparity between the mundane and pragmatic character of the request (finding a job, seeking help for a domestic problem, curing an ailment) and the ineffectuality or outrageousness of the techniques and recommended solutions to the "problem."

One of the most memorable sketches that involves escalation and affective excess begins innocently with a couple seated in a restaurant. The husband discovers a dirty fork on the table and reports the offending utensil to the waiter. News of the dirty fork travels up the hierarchy of the restaurant from the waiter to the manager, to the chef, and then to the owner. The couple never gets a clean fork or a meal, but instead must listen to personal confessions by the staff and is threatened with murder by the enraged chef. Finally, the owner, melodramatically "confesses" all his shortcomings and his misfortunes, concluding his recital with the statement "I want to apologize, humbly, deeply and sincerely." He then commits suicide with the fork. The mundane event of a dirty fork has systematically escalated into a drama of major proportions, and as anticlimax, the husband tells the wife that it was fortunate he didn't report the dirty knife.

“The Funniest Joke in the World” is another instance of the Pythons’ chain reaction and escalation comedy, where the gag overflows the immediate encounter and melodramatically inflates incidents until they far exceed their immediate import. Initially, the skit involves a man who dies of laughing after having created the world’s funniest joke. His wife reads it and expires as well, as do the police. Thus the joke begins its itinerary through various strata of society until it comes into the hands of the British military. After laborious attempts to translate the English joke into German, the British use the joke as a secret weapon against the Nazis, who consequently die laughing. The skit also relies on a number of other comic devices, not the least of which is the polyglot character of the Python sketches, in this case the alternation between the German and English languages. The intertextuality draws on a host of myths about the superiority and culturally sustaining nature of British humor.

The Pythons’ technique of undermining clichés through inversion is further illustrated in “Working-Class Playwright,” a sketch that involves a conflict between Dad (Chapman) and son Ken (Idle), as Mum (Jones) vainly tries to reconcile the

The *Flying Circus*’ Skirmish with Sentiment

quarreling pair. The sketch seems an inversion of stereotypical representations of social class, characteristic of novels such as D. H. Lawrence's *Sons and Lovers*, that highlights the deep social and cultural differences between an artistic son and his miner father. The characters invoke the melodramatic formulas of *Masterpiece Theatre* and the more popular television domestic dramas. In the Python sketch, the son, a coal miner dressed like a business or professional person, arrives home and argues with his father, a writer of plays and poems who is dressed like a miner. Dad tells son Ken, "I like yer fancy suit. Is that what they're wearing up in Yorkshire now?" Ken responds, "It's just an ordinary suit, Father. . . . It's all I've got apart from the overalls." Dad criticizes Ken for his "fancy bloody talk since you left London" and enumerates to his son the hardships of his own work as a writer: "What do you know about getting up at five o'clock in t'mornings to fly to Paris . . . back at the Old Vic for drinks at twelve, sweating the day through press interviews, television interviews and getting back here at ten to wrestle with the problem of a homosexual nymphomaniac drug addict. . . . That's a full working day, lad, and don't you forget it."

Ken finally shouts at the father: "I'll tell you what's wrong with you. Your head is addled with novels and poems. . . . One day you'll realize that there's more to life than culture—there's dirt, and smoke, and good honest sweat." Through a reversal of generational and work roles, the sketch inverts and undermines clichés associated with social class. The son speaks in the educated tones of the bourgeoisie, and the father describes his profession in terms of manual labor. The long-suffering and ineffectual mother, played by Jones, intervenes to calm both father and son: "Oh, don't shout at the boy, father" and "Oh, Ken. Be careful. You know what he's like after a few novels." This sketch goes far beyond parody, exhibiting the multifarious character of Python comic techniques in its drawing on intertextuality, inversion, cross-dressing, explosion of clichés, and escalation of affect.

Recycling Literature, Drama, Cinema, and Art

The *Flying Circus*' sketches drew heavily on canonical works of drama, literature, and film by such authors as Shakespeare, Proust, and Brontë, but emptied them of their revered mode of presentation and interpretation, often turning them into nonsense. Two of the most striking of such transformations are the Pythons' renditions of Emily Brontë's *Wuthering Heights* and Shakespeare's *Julius Caesar*. Through coded language and intertitles, the Python versions of these classical works deflate their affect and reduce the texts to truisms. By transposing novel and play into code and depriving them of the polysemic character of literary language, the Pythons pursue their preoccupation with the vicissitudes of written, spoken, and visual language. As in "The All-England Summarize Proust Contest," in which contestants must reduce *Remembrance of Things Past* to a half-minute, the two sketches ridicule the appropriation of canonical cultural texts for mass cultural consumption: in the Python context, it is not necessary to know the language of these works but only to know of them, a feature that also relates to the "sound byte" aspects of media culture.

The sketches also highlight the absurdity of the media's often seeking "new" forms to make older artistic works accessible to audiences. Once again, the Pythons challenge the pretentiousness of television (particularly the BBC and public television) in their recycling of masterpieces as an ostensible means to "elevate" lowbrow taste to the level of "middlebrow" culture. The sketches invite entry into the more serious dimensions of Python silliness. These sketches of classic texts are self-reflexive about relations among the arts, television, and especially the BBC, in insisting on the importance of "masterpieces." They offer insights into the more serious dimensions of Python silliness as a challenge to the clichés of ordinary discourses and a sign that not everything merits high seriousness and reverence. The sketches expose the pretentiousness of television in its recycling of masterpieces as a supposed means to "elevate" taste, deflecting lowbrow inclinations, and as a counter to the banality of much programming. In its union of high and popular culture through invoking and then altering canonical literary, artistic, and cinematic forms, in reducing and transforming art works to "zaniness" or nonsense, the *Flying Circus*, through these inverted and crazy images of the world turned upside down, offers the viewer the opportunity to question received forms.

Shakespeare's work plays a prominent role in this world of nonsense. Allusions to Shakespeare are interspersed throughout the series, including various incarnations of *Hamlet* and multiple references to Shakespearian acting. For example, one sketch features a hospital to cure overacting, particularly bad Shakespearean actors addicted to declaiming the line from *Richard III*: "A horse, a horse. My kingdom for a horse." Physicians examine these benighted actors in various stages of ranting until one of them, played by Idle, is selected for showing signs of "improvement" in his expression. Now he recites the line, in equally bad acting, without any affect. In another outrageous Shakespearian "performance," the viewer is privileged to watch "The First Underwater Production of *Measure for Measure*." Actors emerging from the sea deliver the lines of the play and then disappear again into the water.

Cinema is not exempt from Python tampering. The "French Subtitled Film" parodies the style of French New Wave cinema. The sketch takes place in a rubbish dump.

The dialogue is minimal as Stig (Jones) and "Girl" (Cleveland) exchange a banal dialogue composed of one-liners. Stig tells the Girl, "Je suis révolutionnaire," accompanied by the intertitle "I am a revolutionary," whereupon her response is a simple "Oh." When the pair meets again, the sketch culminates in images of war as a cabbage floats from the Girl's hands into the air in slow motion. Phil (Idle), an announcer, interrupts the running of the film, describing it pompously with such clichés as "portraying the breakdown of communication in our modern society" and "in a brilliantly conceived montage, Longueur [the name assigned to the director] mercilessly exposes the violence underlying our society." The sketch mimes the cryptic and disjunctive style of New Wave cinema and the tendency of reviewers to uncritically elevate this cinematic form and cinema, generally through pompous and inflated interpretation. Moreover, the choice of the name "Longueur" suggests a tendency of this kind of filmmaking toward slowness and tediousness.

Recycling Classics: *Wuthering Heights* in Semaphore

An assault on clichéd conceptions of classical art takes place in an art gallery among the "masterpieces" of such artists as Millais, Rodin, Gauguin, and Gainsborough as two critics pompously "interpret" paintings. The first critic (Palin), standing in front of a Titian canvas, gushes, "Aren't they marvelous? The strength and boldness . . . life and power of these colors," and the second critic (Idle) adds, "This must be Titian's masterpiece." The first critic rejoins: "Oh, indeed—if only for the composition alone. The strength of those foreground figures—the firmness of the line," and the second critic responds, "Yes, the confidence of the master at the height of his powers." Their comments parody and inflate the academic jargon found in museum captions and art books. Thanks to Gilliam's fanciful animation, the paintings are more "alive" than the critics who discuss the works. By contrast, the figures in the paintings call a strike to protest their situation, leaving their appointed places one by one in the paintings (through animation cutouts), joining their other famous painted comrades on the street and carrying signs expressing their grievances. The idea of paintings coming to life and engaging in political action constitutes another form of Python hyperbole through endowing inanimate objects with life.

Language, Words, Sense, and Nonsense

The uses and abuses of language play a prominent role in most of the sketches. Often the play on words seems nonsensical, bearing no relation whatever to meaning. In some instances, the words are encrypted in sign language, anagrams, or syntactical distortion. In still others, the interaction between two characters relies on the refusal of one character to understand the words of the other by confusing, deforming, or willfully misunderstanding the words. The emphasis on mutilated forms of language reinforces a major philosophical issue in the *Flying Circus*, that the illogicality or madness of the contemporary world is revealed through pathological forms of communication. The carnivalesque character of the programs derives from inverting what passes for normality; turning upside down categories of normality and pathology, sense and nonsense; and making it possible to view the world differently. The artful and transgressive forms of comedy in the *Flying Circus* validate Michel Foucault's examination of how art can open "a void, a moment of silence, a question without an answer, [and] provokes a breach without reconciliation where the world is forced to question itself."[68]

The "pathology" of language is also present in "E. Henry Thripshaw's Disease." Burrows (Palin) visits a physician, Thripshaw (Cleese), and describes his complaint thus: "My particular prob, or buglem bear, I've had for ages. For years, I've had it for donkeys." This condition "is so embarrassing when my wife and I go to an orgy." Of course, the physician does not address the disease but regards it as an opportunity to become famous by publicizing the "disease that is so rare, it hasn't got a name" on television programs such as "Call My Bluff." Another "pathology" of language is manifest in the sketches involving "The Man Who Says Words in the Wrong Order" ("Good morning, Doctor. Nice year for the time of day"), "The Man Who Only Speaks the Ends of Words," "The Man Who Only Speaks the Beginnings of Words," "The Man Who Speaks Only the Middles of Words," and "The Man Who Speaks in Anagrams." This final sketch ends with a quarrel between the man who speaks in anagrams (Idle) and the interviewer (Palin). After distorting and intoning the famous line from "Ring Kichard the Thrid," "A shroe, a shroe. My dingkom for a shroe!" the interviewer says, "Ah, King Richard, yes . . .

but surely that's not an anagram, that's a spoonerism." The man responds, "If you're going to split hairs, I'm going to piss off."

The difficulty of a speaker struggling to find the right words takes many forms. For example, the sketches involving a televised murder mystery accentuate the linguistic incompetence of the detectives. The setting is the predictable drawing room. The suspects are grouped around the sofa and in front of the fireplace as the inspector, dressed in a trench coat, paces and ineptly interrogates the group. In the "Agatha Christie" sketch, Inspector Muffin (Palin) struggles with malapropisms or is completely at a loss for the word he needs to conduct his investigation. The sketch begins like a familiar crime detection program, but the conventional aspects of the genre dissolve the language of the detective. He becomes enmeshed in convoluted language and falls deeper and deeper into a linguistic crisis about the proper form of the questions he's supposed to be asking, stumbling over the selection and order of nouns and verbs

The Paintings Fight Back: "Art Strike"

and where to place adverbial phrases. Muffin enters and announces to the assembled group: "All right, don't anybody move, there's been a murder." The mother asks, "A murder?" and he says, "No . . . not a murder . . . no, what's like a murder only begins with B?" The son responds, "Birmingham"; the doctor, "Burnley"; and Muffin says, "That's right. . . . There's been a Burnley." Increasingly, his syntax unravels, and as he gets verbally lost, the sketch shifts from a whodunit to a linguistic farce.

The *Flying Circus*' transgressive dissection of language as a conventional gauge of sense and meaning is evident throughout the many programs. For example, as a television personality who is a commentator on world affairs, Palin hosts a show called "Spectrum." The show begins with typical grandiose fanfare and an overhead image of a rainbow as the logo for the program. Palin's introduction to the program suggests that it will be looking at "what's going on." Pompously, he says, "What are the figures, what are the facts . . ." Chapman, standing before a graph, rattles off different percentages about the population as Palin comments, "Telling figures indeed, but what do these figures mean? What do they mean to me? What do they mean to the average man in the street?" And now the requisite "expert," Professor Tiddles of Leeds University, is asked what he thinks and intones, "Too early to tell." Palin then holds up cards to cue the audience to the "meaning of words" and then says, "What does this mean?" Turning to a cricketer (Idle) for advice, he gets none, and then asks, "What does this mean? What am I doing? What am I saying? What am I going to do next?" In one fell swoop, the sketch has emptied documentation of expertise, calling attention to the pseudo-authoritative voice of the television commentator and the emptiness of linguistic content.

The problem of finding the right word to convey a request is often linked to differences in styles of speaking, attributable to social class. In one sketch, "Fish License,"

Praline (Cleese) seeks to buy a license for his pet halibut but has difficulty explaining his request to a post office clerk. He informs the clerk, "I'd like to buy a license for my pet fish, Eric," and the man responds, "How did you know my name was Eric?" Thus begins a verbal encounter between the two men that escalates with each request made by Praline and each negative response by the clerk. The sketch hinges on Praline's insistence that there is indeed such a thing as a fish license just as there are dog licenses and, he claims, "cat licenses." The clerk repeats, "You are a loony." This nonsensical dialogue appears to involve the petitioner's pretentiousness not only in asking for a license for his halibut but in his tendency to invoke inflated language such as "Dame Fortune smiles upon my next postal adventure" and his reference to the "late, great Marcel Proust who had a 'addock, if you're calling the author of 'A La recherche du temps perdu' a loony, I shall have to ask you to set outside." As in other sketches, there is no "resolution" and no punch line, and it is an instance of a sketch that is a transition to another sketch, triggered by Praline's appeal to the Lord Mayor for a "signed statement that there is no such thing as a "fish license." "Fish License" plays with various Python motifs concerning language. As Palin observed, "Piscatorial images were very strong. We had an instinct that the word 'haddock' was quite funny or 'halibut.'"[69]

These skits draw on a familiar Python motif, one that makes humor out of privation and incongruity and points to the disjunction between "signs" and the objects to which they refer. The relation between salespeople and customers, like so many interactions in other skits, is one of misrepresentation, evasion, and circumlocution on the part of the person in charge. The behavior of the customer or petitioner is characterized by incomprehension, persistence, and finally desperation.

Miscommunication is evident in the sketch "Registry Office," where a man (Jones) comes in for a marriage license. He asks the registrar, "Er, excuse me, I want to get married," and the registrar responds, "I'm afraid I'm already married." This type of miscommunication is further complicated in "The Dirty Hungarian Phrasebook" sketch, in which Cleese, with a phrase book in hand, comes into a tobacconist's shop, presumably to buy cigarettes. A rolling caption reads, "IN 1970, THE BRITISH EMPIRE LAY IN RUINS, FOREIGN NATIONALS FREQUENTED THE STREETS—MANY OF THEM HUNGARIANS—(NOT THE STREETS—THE FOREIGN NATIONALS). ANYWAY, MANY OF THESE HUNGARIANS WENT INTO TOBACCONIST'S SHOPS TO BUY CIGARETTES." Jones, as the tobacconist, tries to explain to the Hungarian what kind of shop he runs, but the Hungarian, relying on his phrase book appears unable to understand the tobacconist's response.

After telling the tobacconist, "I will not buy this 'tobacconist,' it is scratched" and other bizarre associations, he shifts into a seductive register saying, "Do you waaaant . . . to come back to my place, bouncy, bouncy." When the tobacconist reads a phrase from the phrase book, Cleese punches Jones, and a police officer enters. Now the phrase Cleese reads becomes more sexually explicit: "Ah, you have beautiful thighs. . . . Drop your panties, Sir William; I cannot wait 'til lunch time. . . . My nipples explode with delight!" In this case, the Hungarian's uses of language do not seem inappropriate or incomprehensible in their explicit references to "naughty" sexuality. In fact, the sketch, in shifting gears, does not seem too concerned with simple mistranslation but with something more complicated, involving the usual Python undermining of reductive commonsense explanations of language use. The sketch also connects language to censorship and policing, appropriately continuing later in the courtroom. This sketch, like the one involving a Python list of words not to be used on BBC television, underscores the ever-present role of censorship concerning sexuality.

A different way of addressing language involves connections between verbal and visual language, or rather interference, in any expectation of their union and equivalence, as in the "translation" of *Wuthering Heights* into semaphore language, the staging of *Julius Caesar* with an Aldis lamp, the presentation of Wacky Queen Victoria through animation that becomes a silent film, or in the spoof "French Subtitled Film." Various sketches, particularly those in the animated sequences, utilize the nonverbal language of groans, squeals, and squawks. Also the transposition from verbal to gestural language is evident in other sketches: for example, a courtroom drama enacted through a game of charades in which the cross-examination and the verdict are rendered through gestures. These sketches are further instances of the serious character of Python silliness. The sundering of word and image indicates a tension between verbal and visual images and undermines reassurance about the trustworthiness of language.

In the sketch "Woody and Tinny Words," featuring Chapman as the father, Cleveland as the daughter, and Idle as the mother, a family is seated in a 1920s drawing room with cook, maid, butler, and chauffeur standing silently behind them. In a lengthy discussion, the family debates the merits of "wood" over "tin" for croquet hoops as the dialogue moves from one word to the next, playing always on the words *tin* and *wood*, introducing confusion between words and things.

> Father: Tin, tin, tin.
>
> (The daughter bursts into tears.)
>
> Mother: Oh, don't say "tin" to Rebecca, you know how it upsets her.
>
> Father: (to the daughter) Sorry, old horse.
>
> Mother: Sausage . . . there's a good woody sort of word, sausage . . . gorn.

Daughter: Antelope.

Father: Where? On the lawn? (he picks up a rifle)

Daughter: No, no, daddy, just the word.

The sketch continues in this zany fashion, invoking the connotations of various words that are substantial or insubstantial, trustworthy or "naughty," until Father introduces the word *intercourse*.

> Father: No, no—the word, "intercourse"—good and woody . . . inter . . . course . . . pert . . . pert thighs . . . botty, botty, botty . . . (the mother leaves the room) . . . erogenous . . . zone . . . concubine . . . erogenous zone! Loose woman . . . erogenous zone . . .
>
> (The mother returns and throws a bucket of water over him.)
>
> Father: Oh thank you . . . dear . . . you know, it's a funny thing, dear . . . all the naughty words sound woody.

This sketch captures elements central to the Pythons' play with language involving seemingly disconnected associations and non sequiturs that blur the borders between sense and nonsense. The viewer is aware of the servants standing behind the seated family, observing the conversation in silence. Their nonparticipation in the scene further highlights the nonsensical dialogue that is not merely vapid silliness; instead, the dialogue captures not only class distinctions in language but also the tenuous character of meaning.

Many of the sketches portray commercial negotiations gone awry. In "Dead Parrot," a customer (Cleese) enters a parrot shop and complains to the owner (Palin) that he has been sold a dead parrot. The owner denies that the parrot is dead. He insists that the bird is only resting, offering a psychological explanation: as a Norwegian parrot, the bird is homesick for the fjords. Exasperated, the customer takes the bird, dashes it to the floor, and shouts in exasperation: "This parrot is no more. It has ceased to be. It's expired and gone to see its maker. This is a late parrot. It's a stiff. Bereft of life, it rests in peace. If you hadn't nailed it to the perch, it would be pushing up the daisies. It's rung down the curtain and joined the choir invisible. It's an ex-parrot." Now the problem of replacing the parrot becomes complicated, because the owner claims he is out of parrots and tries to sell the customer another "animal" that he can "design." The episode relies on the stubborn resistance on the part of the owner to acknowledge the parrot as dead and the desperation on the part of the customer as he tries to make himself understood, convince the salesman that the parrot is indeed dead, and gain restitution. Cleese's speech to the salesman relies on euphemisms for death as well as a frustrating recourse to repetition, reinforcement, and acceleration of terminology. In addition, the more he insists, the more he reveals his frustration with the stolid resistance of the salesman.

Another instance of fraudulent commerce involves Palin as an encyclopedia salesman who finds a novel way to gain the attention and confidence of a potential customer who mistrusts salespeople. She repeatedly insists that he is a salesman but then succumbs to the absurd explanation of his motive for entry—he is not a salesman but a robber. However, when he enters the house, he reverts to his encyclopedia sales pitch. In making a connection between door-to-door encyclopedia salespeople and robbers, and by means of Palin's devious ploy to represent himself as a robber and not as a salesman, the sketch suggests not only that such salespeople are devious but also that they are robbers, if not worse than robbers.

Common Sense and Audience Response

Woven throughout the *Flying Circus* are the "Vox Pops," the voices of the "people" designated by the Pythons as representing commonsensical responses to events. These responses are associated in the series with a commonsense view of the world expressed in terms of moral aphorisms, reductive explanation, nostalgia for bygone times, and a sense of righteousness often couched in terms of good and bad taste. The Pythons use various figures such as the "Gumbies" and the "Pepperpots" as well as letters from critics of the program to exemplify common sense. A key role is played in the sketches of letters by disgruntled, morally offended patrons, clergymen, and military "men" (of uncertain gender). These "disclaimers" become a further way in which the episodes reach out to focus on the vulnerability of both the medium and its spectators.

"This Is a Late Parrot"

Many of the "complaints" have to do with questions of perceived "bad taste." Sometimes the complaints concern the presentation of sexuality, and sometimes they take issue with the style of the sketches, particularly stressing the unfunny dimensions of a particular sketch. A knight with a plucked chicken will appear and hit the characters, thus ending the sketch. At other times, a Python will appear to announce that the sketch was "stupid" or tasteless, and it is stopped in midstream (often to return in a later episode). Letters from viewers are another device to call attention to the relations among producers, spectators, and authorities from the BBC, who will be invoked, even mocked, throughout various episodes. Although in the first episodes censorship was not a major issue, increasingly it became a problem as certain viewers objected to the "bad taste" of the Pythons, specifically their use of such subjects as undertakers, corpses, religion, sex, and violence. Instead of toning down the material to suit their critics, the Pythons acknowledged the "offenses," incorporated them as further sources of humor, and underlined, even escalated, the irreverence.

In one of the sketches, titled "Apology," a voice-over reads a rolling caption, disavowing "disgusting" material:

> 1st Voice-Over: The BBC would like to apologize to everyone in the world for the last item [Sam Peckinpah's "Salad Days"]. It was disgusting and bad and thoroughly disobedient and please don't bother to phone up because we know it was really tasteless, but they really don't mean it and they do all come from broken homes and have very unhappy personal lives. . . . And please don't write in either because the BBC is going through an unhappy phase at the moment—what with its father dying and the mortgage and BBC 2 going out with men.
>
> 2nd Voice-over: The BBC would like to deny the last

apology. It is very happy at home and BBC 2 is bound to go through this phase.

In addition, the *Flying Circus* takes aim at the constraints and absurdity of common sense through specific characters. The "Gumbies," for example, are another Python strategy to assault the common sense of audience response. Increasingly familiar characters in the *Flying Circus* series, the "Gumbies" were part of the recurrent but not always predictable patterns of the episodes. The "Gumby" is "a brainless sub-human with rolled-up trousers, round steel-rimmed spectacles, braces, a small moustache, and a handkerchief with the corners knotted as a head piece."[70] One of the roles of the "Gumbies" is to embody the problematic character of television as it condescends to "elevate" the "man on the street." As the Pythons played them, the "Gumbies" not only invoked television's tendency to rely increasingly on untutored "audience" responses but also, as the Pythons portrayed them, became part of a world of automata characteristic of modern life, incarnations of nightmares of mediocrity, misinformation, and even violence.

Often throughout the forty-five episodes the properties of common sense are highlighted—through the complaining letter writers introduced after or during sketches, the "art critics," the "Gumbies," and the "women on the street." These characters know what they like and what they don't like. They express their outrage against the flouting of conventional wisdom and morality or take pride in expressing themselves as the voices of sanity and common sense, while also exposing their ridiculousness. For example, in "Gumby Crooner," Professor R. J. Gumby, an advocate of the "good old days," intones: "Well, I think TV's killed real entertainment. In the old days we used to make our own fun. At Christmas parties I used to strike myself on the head repeatedly with blunt instruments while crooning."

Other than dramatizing judgments on the moral or immoral character of television, the *Flying Circus* focused on television viewing in the home. Not only are characters interviewed by announcers on the street about their opinions on various subjects, including television, but they are also shown sitting before the radio or TV in anticipation of a particular program. This viewing is often conveyed through the Pepperpots, with names derived from elementary logic such as Mrs. Premise, Mrs. Conclusion, Mrs. Thing, and Mrs. Entity. In "The Death of Mary, Queen of Scots," they listen to the violent sound effects of the drama "specially adapted for radio by Bernard Hollowood and Brian London. And now Radio 4 will explode." (The radio explodes.) At this point, the First Pepperpot (Chapman) says to the second Pepperpot (Cleese), "We'll have to watch the telly then," and the women change their viewing position to face a TV set. The women then gaze at a penguin sitting atop the TV and ruminate on its origins.

"Taking Off" on Censorship

First Pepperpot: Per'aps it's from the zoo.

Second Pepperpot: Which zoo?

First Pepperpot: (angrily) 'Ow should I know which zoo it's from. I'm not Doctor Bloody Bronowski!

Second Pepperpot: Oo's Bloody Bronowski?

First Pepperpot: He knows everything.

Second Pepperpot: Ooh, I wouldn't like that, it would take all the mystery out of life.

When the television goes on, the news announcer says, "Hello! Well, it's just after eight o'clock, and time for the penguin on top of your television set to explode." The first Pepperpot says, "'Ow did 'e know that was going to happen?" and the man on the television responds, "It was an inspired guess." Other than identifying the domestic setting for television and associating it primarily, though not exclusively, with women, the sketch also dramatizes viewers' familiarity with television personalities in allusions to such programs as *The Ascent of Man* (television, 1973), hosted by Bronowski, or *The Brains Trust* (radio, 1941, and television, 1955–61). In the *Flying Circus*, not only do viewers talk to the box, but television personalities often talk directly to them and even occasionally leave the box to enter the home, another Python strategy for blurring lines between real and imaginary worlds and for situating the spectator in an indeterminate zone of meaning.

The *Flying Circus* Revisited

Monty Python's Flying Circus continues to be rebroadcast, and videos and DVDs of all of the episodes have been released for consumer purchase. The series has maintained its cult status as new generations discover the Pythons. Books—biographies and critical studies—appear regularly by and on the individual members of the group. The Pythons appear in reunions and individually on television talk shows in the United States and elsewhere. The popularity of the series internationally contradicts the claim that comedy appeals exclusively to a national constituency, given the cultural and linguistic idiosyncrasy with which it is often associated.

In 1989, reviewer Andrew Clifford wrote in anticipation of a BBC "Monty Python Special" and in response to a book on the *Flying Circus*,

> Monty Python is 20 years old. The team's first show was broadcast on BBC2 on 5 October 1969. For a while the show languished on the BBC's second channel. Seemingly watched only by those keen on a little extra Call-My-Bluff activity. Soon it had a cult following. . . . Twenty years on and the best of Monty Python still outshines its imitators in sheer comic inventiveness. No other comedians have inspired such a devoted, indeed virtually addicted following.[71]

In 1994, a Comedy Central *Python-a-thon* was described as "remarkably fresh."[72] And in 1998, at the Aspen Reunion of the group minus Chapman (d. 1989), the *Flying Circus* was lauded as "groundbreaking comedy and groundbreaking television . . . the group created countless quotable bits that have entered comedy history."[73]

In 1998, reviewer Anna Mulrine, stressing the influential role of the Pythons, wrote in *U.S. News and World Report*, "Weaned on Pythons' unorthodox blend of the surreal, the silly, and the cerebral, today's comedians are looking to Python as they rebel against the formula of sitcoms, the convention of sitcoms, and the tired repetition of shows like *Saturday Night Live*. . . . *Flying Circus* marked a revolution in both form and content of American television as it had in Britain from 1969 through 1974."[74] This "revolution . . . in form and content" was not merely due to the range and variety of topics introduced by the shows but due to the excessive and "cerebral" ways in which these topics were treated. The accepted world was turned on its head through hyperbole and reversal of expectations. The Pythons used these strategies of comedy to call attention to the role of institutions—medicine, psychiatry, the family, the state's administration of social life, the uses and abuses of history, and especially the disciplining of the sexual body through existing social formations.

Many sketches involve the diverse ways in which language, individual and social behavior, and physical appearance are wrenched from their conventional contexts. In the reiterative emphasis on bodily gesture through the Pythons' stylized movement and animation, the *Flying Circus* highlighted the importance of gesture as a means of communicating knowledge often blocked in reigning channels of communication. Philosopher Giorgio Agamben has described the gesture as "always a gesture of not being able to figure out something in language; it is always a gag in the proper meaning of the term, indicating first of all something that could be put into your mouth to hinder speech, as well as in the sense of the actor's improvisation meant to compensate a loss of memory or an inability to speak."[75] Through the "gag," by means of gesture and animation, the *Flying Circus* was able to jar uncritical common sense, holding it up to scrutiny and invoking a forgotten world where silence reigns. The Python comedy repeatedly invoked not only the legal practice of censorship but also the multifarious forms of indirect censorship that are expressed in the banalities of institutional discourses and exercised in every aspect of social and cultural life.

The "unorthodox," the "something different" (to borrow the Pythons' own repeated slogan) that further marked the outstanding contribution of the *Flying Circus* to television was not only its tendency to make visible the properties of the televisual but also its ability to maintain its role as pleasurable, even pedagogical, entertainment. In short, the episodes of the series can be fruitfully studied as a text on the nature of television in its cavalier uses of time, segmentation, and patterns of programming, including news reporting, educational programming, cinema, musical performance, and theater.

The originality of the series resided not only in the wide-ranging subjects that the group chose to portray as endemic to contemporary culture but also in its self-conscious contentiousness with the existing forms of television as inane entertainment and vacuous information. Through the various sketches, the viewer is treated to a jamming of clichéd and conventionalized modes of apprehending the world through televisual images. The terms adopted to describe the *Flying Circus*—surreal, bizarre, zany, silly, and so on—would seem to situate the program in a postmodern world of fragmentation, spatial and temporal discontinuity, the abandonment of history, and the meaninglessness of language as a transparent means of communication. For example, in praise of the uniqueness of the series, television critic Jeff MacGregor declared,

> For ardent fans, the 45 original episodes remain a high point in the history of comedy television. There hasn't been another sketch-driven ensemble series anywhere before or since that so completely succeeded in what it set out to do. Its slippery logic and postmodern self-awareness pioneered a style that has never successfully been imitated. Its joyful and singular appreciation of both lowbrow and antic vaudeville and a high-minded theater of the absurd is a model of the form.[76]

By citing the pastiche qualities, the mixing of high and low cultures, and the self-reflexive dimensions of the *Flying*

Circus, MacGregor situates Python comedy within a postmodern context. Indeed, the *Flying Circus* invokes many of the characteristics attributed to postmodern production: namely its focus on parody, intertextuality, eclecticism, mixing and contaminating of artistic and cultural forms as well as borders between the real and imaginary. These qualities are identified with the "society of the spectacle," in which the image has assumed the status of master of reality. If the *Flying Circus* is exemplary of postmodern cultural production, as some critics such as MacGregor claim, the Pythons' contribution can better be understood as aware, but critical, of the postmodern condition.

The exclusive attention to the formal dimensions of the series by reviewers and critics disregards the possibility that a case can be made for the *Flying Circus* as diagnosing the postmodern condition rather than merely capitalizing on its stylistic tendencies. The *Flying Circus* creatively used the technological resources of television to call attention to the potential looseness and malleability of the medium, thereby offering productive insights into what critics have termed the "society of the spectacle." In what the shows selected to portray, they encouraged the spectator to interact critically with the tendency of the culture via television to induce distraction, forgetfulness, and habituation.

NOTES

1. Hendrik Herzberg, "Onward and Upward with Arts: Naughty Bits," *New Yorker*, March 29, 1976, 80.
2. Ibid., 72.
3. Ibid.
4. Ibid., 84.
5. Ibid., 86.
6. Anthony Smith, *Television: An International History* (Oxford: Oxford University Press, 1998), 2.
7. David Sterritt and Lucille Rhodes, "Monty Python Lust for Glory," *Cineaste* 26, no. 14 (Fall 2001): 6.
8. Roger Wilmut, *From Fringe to Flying Circus* (London: Methuen, 1980), 195.
9. David Morgan, *Monty Python Speaks* (London: Fourth Estate, 1999), 10.
10. T. J. F., "Michael Palin," *Current Biography* (February 2000): 59–64.
11. John Cleese, Terry Gilliam, Michael Palin, Eric Idle, Terry Jones, and the Estate of Graham Chapman, *The Pythons: Autobiography by the Pythons* (New York: St. Martin's Press, 2003), 152.
12. Tom Nairn, *The Break-Up of Britain: Crisis and Neonationalism* (London: New Left, 1977).
13. Alan Asked and Chris Cook, *Post-War Britain: A Political History* (Harmondsworth, Eng.: Penguin, 1990), 250–52.

14. John Hill, *Sex, Class and Realism: British Cinema 1956–63* (London: BFI, 1986), 10.
15. Steve Neale and Frank Krutnik, *Popular Film and Television Comedy.* (London: Routledge, 1990), 207.
16. Sarah Street, *Transatlantic Crossings: British Feature Films in the USA* (New York: Continuum, 2002), 182.
17. Wilmut, *From Fringe to Flying Circus*, 57.
18. Edward Said, *Representations of the Intellectual: The 1993 Reith Lectures* (New York: Vintage, 1994), ix.
19. Anthony Smith, "License and Liberty: Public Service Broadcasting in Britain," in *The BBC and Public Service Broadcasting*, ed. Colin MacCabe and Olivia Stewart, 49 (Manchester: Manchester University Press, 1986).
20. Ibid., 10.
21. Geoffrey Wheatcroft, "Who Needs the BBC?" *Atlantic Monthly* (March 2001): 2.

22. Wilmut, *From Fringe to Flying Circus*, 62.
23. The Minister of War, John Profumo, was exposed as having an affair with a woman, Christine Keeler, who was also sexually involved with a Soviet diplomat. See the film *Scandal* (1989) and Asked and Cook, *Post-War Britain*, 185–87.
24. Wilmut, *From Fringe to Flying Circus*, 72.
25. David Frost, *An Autobiography*, vol. 1, *From Congregations to Audiences* (London: HarperCollins, 1994), 47.
26. Ibid., 181.
27. Colin MacCabe and Olivia Stewart, eds., *The BBC and Public Service Broadcasting* (Manchester: Manchester University Press, 1986), 34–35.
28. Robert Hewison, *Monty Python: The Case Against* (New York: Grove Press, 1981), 15.
29. Ibid., 29.
30. Ibid., 21–22.
31. Ibid., 24.
32. Wilmut, *From Fringe to Flying Circus*, 207.
33. Jeffrey Miller, *Something Completely Different: British Television and American Culture* (Minneapolis: University of Minnesota Press, 2000), 18.
34. Ibid.
35. Asa Briggs, *The BBC: The First Fifty Years* (Oxford: Oxford University Press, 1985), 346.

36. Arthur Unger, "Monty Python Invades U.S. Commercial TV," *Christian Science Monitor*, October 2, 1975, 22.
37. Wilmut, *From Fringe to Flying Circus*, 228.
38. Ibid.
39. Stanley Reynolds, "Bargain for the BBC," *London Times*, September 16, 1970, 13.
40. Ellen Bishop, "Bakhtin, Carnival, and Comedy: The New Grotesque in *Monty Python and the Holy Grail*," *Film Criticism* 15, no. 1 (1990): 49–64.
41. Gilles Deleuze, *The Logic of Sense*, trans. Mark Lester (New York: Columbia University Press, 1990), 74–82.
42. Anna Mulrine, "Off to the Flying Circus: Comedy's New Stars Silly-Walk in the Footsteps of Monty Python," *U.S. News and World Report*, March 23, 1998, 64.
43. Cleveland Amory, "Monty Python's Flying Circus," *TV Guide*, May 17, 1975, 32.
44. Unger, "Monty Python Invades U.S. Commercial TV," 22.
45. Veronica Geng, "The Complete Monty Python's Flying Circus: All the Words," *New Republic*, April 23, 1990, 33.
46. Northrop Frye, *Anatomy of Criticism: Four Essays* (Princeton, N.J.: Princeton University Press, 1957), 224.
47. John O. Thompson, *Monty Python: Complete and Utter Theory of the Grotesque* (London: BFI, 1982), 8.
48. Frye, *Anatomy of Criticism*, 309.
49. Andrew Clifford, "Caught in the Act," *New Statesman and Society*, September 29, 1989, 42.
50. Marcia Landy, *British Genres, Cinema and Society, 1930–1960* (Princeton, N.J.: Princeton University Press), 1991.
51. Marion Jordan, "Carry On . . . Follow That Stereotype," in *British Cinema History*, ed. James Curran and Vincent Porter, 324–25 (London: Weidenfeld and Nicolson, 1983).
52. Ibid., 29.
53. Wilmut, *From Fringe to Flying Circus*, 198.
54. Guy Debord, *The Society of the Spectacle*, trans. Donald Nicholson-Smith (New York: Zone, 1994).
55. Jean Baudrillard, *Screened Out*, trans. Chris Turner (London: Verso, 2002), 176.
56. Ibid., 90.
57. Wilmut, *From Fringe to Flying Circus*, 198.
58. Neale and Krutnik, *Popular Film and Television Comedy*, 205.

59. Smith, *Television*, 2.
60. Ibid., 1.
61. Reynolds, "Bargain for the BBC," 13.
62. Morgan, *Monty Python Speaks*, 83.
63. Wilmut, *From Fringe to Flying Circus*, 207.
64. Reynolds, "Bargain for the BBC," 13.
65. Anthony Davis, *Television: The First Forty Years* (London: Independent Television Productions, 1976), 101.
66. Wilmut, *From Fringe to Flying Circus*, 198.
67. Bill Bryson, "Cleese Up Close," *New York Times Magazine*, December 25, 1988, 15.
68. Michel Foucault, *Madness and Civilization: A History of Insanity in the Age of Reason* (New York: Mentor, 1967), 231.
69. Cleese, Gilliam, Palin, Idle, Jones, and Chapman, *Autobiography*, 185.
70. Wilmut, *From Fringe to Flying Circus*, 202.
71. Clifford, "Caught in the Act," 42.
72. William E. Schmidt, "Still Zany, Python and Cult Turn 25," *New York Times*, September 24, 1994, C13, C20.
73. Bruce Weber, "Something Completely Nostalgic: A Monty Python Reunion, Minus One Slapstick Subversive," *New York Times*, March 9, 1999, E1.
74. Mulrine, "Off to the Flying Circus," 64.
75. Giorgio Agamben, *Means without End: Notes on Politics*, trans. Vincenzo Binetti and Cesare Casarino (Minneapolis: University of Minnesota Press, 2000), 58.
76. Jeff MacGregor, "The Naughty Surreal Pleasures of the 'Python' 6," *New York Times*, June 21, 1998, ARTS 35.

VIDEOGRAPHY AND FILMOGRAPHY

Season 1

October 5, 1969	Sex and Violence
October 12, 1969	Whither Canada?
October 19, 1969	How to Recognize Different Types of Trees from Quite a Long Way Away
October 26, 1969	Owl-Stretching Time
November 16, 1969	Man's Crisis of Identity in the Latter Half of the Twentieth Century
November 23, 1969	The Ant, an Introduction
November 30, 1969	Oh, You're No Fun Anymore
December 7, 1969	The BBC Entry for the Zinc Stoat of Budapest
December 14, 1969	Full Frontal Nudity
December 21, 1969	No title
December 28, 1969	The Royal Philharmonic Orchestra Goes to the Bathroom
January 4, 1970	The Naked Ant
January 11, 1970	Intermission

Season 2

September 15, 1970	Dinsdale
September 22, 1970	The Spanish Inquisition
September 29, 1970	Show 5
October 20, 1970	The Buzz Aldrin Show
October 27, 1970	Live from the Grillomat
November 3, 1970	School Prizes

November 11, 1970	The Attila the Hun Show
November 17, 1970	Archaeology Today
November 24, 1970	How to Recognize Different Parts of the Body
December 1, 1970	Scott of the Antarctic
December 8, 1970	How Not to be Seen
December 15, 1970	Spam
December 22, 1970	Royal Episode 13

Season 3

October 19, 1972	Njorl's Saga
October 26, 1972	Mr. & Mrs. Brian Norris's Ford Popular
November 2, 1972	The Money Programme
November 9, 1972	Blood, Devastation, Death, War and Horror
November 16, 1972	The All-England Summarize Proust Competition
November 23, 1972	The War Against Pornography
November 30, 1972	Salad Days
December 7, 1972	The Cycling Tour
December 14, 1972	The Nude Man
December 21, 1972	E. Henry Thripshaw's Disease
January 4, 1973	Dennis Moore
January 11, 1973	A Book at Bedtime
January 18, 1973	The British Royal Awards Programme

Season 4

October 31, 1974	The Golden Age of Ballooning
November 7, 1974	Michael Ellis
November 14, 1974	Anything Goes, The Light Entertainment War
November 21, 1974	Hamlet
November 28, 1974	Mr. Neutron
December 5, 1974	A Party Political Broadcast on Behalf of the Liberal Party

Special

October, 1973	Monty Python's Fliegender Zirkus

Feature Movies

Monty Python's And Now for Something Completely Different (1971)
Monty Python and the Holy Grail (1975)
Monty Python's Life of Brian (1979)
Monty Python Live at the Hollywood Bowl (1982)
Monty Python's Meaning of Life (1983)

SELECTED BIBLIOGRAPHY

Amory, Cleveland. "Monty Python's Flying Circus." *TV Guide*, May 17, 1975, 32.

Asked, Alan, and Chris Cook. *Post-War Britain: A Political History*. London: Penguin, 1990.

Bakhtin, M. M. *Rabelais and His World*. Trans. Helen Iswolsky. Cambridge, Mass.: MIT Press, 1968.

Barr, Charles. *Ealing Studios*. Woodstock, N.Y.: Overlook, 1980.

Baudrillard, Jean. *Screened Out*. Trans. Chris Turner. London: Verso, 2002.

Bermel, Albert. *Farce: A History from Aristophanes to Woody Allen*. New York: Simon and Schuster, 1982.

Bishop, Ellen. "Bakhtin, Carnival, and Comedy: The New Grotesque in *Monty Python and the Holy Grail*." *Film Criticism* 15, no. 1 (1990): 49–64.

Briggs, Asa. *The BBC: The First Fifty Years*. Oxford: Oxford University Press, 1985.

Brown, Les. "The American Networks." In *Television: An International History*, ed. Anthony Smith with Richard Patterson, 147–62. Oxford: Oxford University Press, 1998.

Bryson, Bill. "Cleese Up Close." *New York Times Magazine*, December 25, 1988, 14–16, 22–25.

Burns, Tom. *The BBC: Public Institution and Private World*. New York: Holmes and Meier, 1977.

Buscombe, Ed, ed. *British Television: A Reader*. London: Oxford University Press, 2000.

Carpenter, Humphrey. *That Was Satire That Was: The Satire Boom of the 1960s*. London: Victor Gollancz, 2000.

Casey, Bernadette, Neil Casey, Ben Calvert, Liam French, and Justin Lewis. *Television Studies: The Key Concepts*. London: Routledge, 2002.

Christie, Ian. *Gilliam on Gilliam*. London: Faber and Faber, 1999.

Cleese, John, Terry Gilliam, Michael Palin, Eric Idle, Terry Jones, and the Estate of Graham Chapman. *The Pythons: Autobiography by the Pythons*. New York: St. Martin's Press, 2003.

Clifford, Andrew. "Caught in the Act." *New Statesman and Society*, September 29, 1989, 42–43.

Corner, John, ed. *Popular Television in Britain: Studies in Cultural History*. London: BFI, 1991.

Davis, Anthony. *Television: The First Forty Years*, London: Independent Television Productions, 1976.

Debord, Guy. *Society of the Spectacle*. Trans. Donald Nicholson-Smith. New York: Zone Books, 1994.

Deleuze, Gilles. *The Logic of Sense*. Trans. Mark Lester. New York: Columbia University Press, 1990.

Dienst, Richard. *Still Life in Real Time: Theory After Television*. Durham, N.C.: Duke University Press, 1995.

Feuer, Jane. "The Concept of Live Television: Ontology as Ideology." In *Regarding Television*, ed. E. Ann Kaplan, 12–21. Frederick, Md.: University Publications of America, 1983.

Foucault, Michel. *Madness and Civilization: A History of Insanity in the Age of Reason*. New York: Mentor, 1967.

French, Sean. "Why Are More People Interested in Norman Mailer's Penis or Martin Amis's Teeth than in Their Books?" *New Statesman*, October 11, 1999, 28.

Frischauer, Willi. *David Frost*. London: Michael Joseph, 1972.

Frost, David. *An Autobiography*. Vol. 1, *From Congregations to Audiences*. London: Harper Collins, 1994.

Frye, Northrop. *Anatomy of Criticism: Four Essays*. Princeton, N.J.: Princeton University Press, 1957.

Geng, Veronica. "The Complete Monty Python's Flying Circus: All the Words." *New Republic*, April 23, 1990, 34.

Gilliam, Terry. *Dark Knights and Holy Fools: The Art and Films of Terry Gilliam*. New York: Universe, 1999.

Gilliatt, Penelope. "Height's Delight." *New Yorker*, May 2, 1988, 41–56.

Glasgow, R. D. V. *Madness, Masks, and Laughter*. Madison, N.J.: Fairleigh Dickinson Press, 1995.

Green, Ian. "Ealing in the Comedy Frame." *British Cinema History*, ed. James Curran and Vincent Porter, 294–303. London: Weidenfeld and Nicolson, 1983.

Herzberg, Hendrik. "Onward and Upward with Arts: Naughty Bits." *New Yorker*, March 29, 1976, 69–86.

Hewison, Robert. *Monty Python: The Case Against*. New York: Grove Press, 1981.

Horn, Andrew. "The Gold Doubloon: Radio Drama and the Narrative Gestalt." In *After Narrative: The Pursuit of Reality and Fiction*, ed. Suva Subramani, 211–23. Auckland, New Zealand: University of the South Pacific, 1990.

Horton, Andrew S., ed. *Comedy/Cinema/Theory*. Berkeley: University of California Press, 1991.

Johnson, Kim Howard. *Life before and after Monty Python: The Solo Flights of the Flying Circus*. New York: St. Martin's Press. 1993.

Jordan, Marion. "Carry On . . . Follow That Stereotype." In *British Cinema History*, ed. James Curran and Vincent Porter, 312–28. London: Weidenfeld and Nicolson, 1983.

Joyrich, Lynne. *Re-viewing Reception: Television, Gender, and Postmodern Culture*. Bloomington: Indiana University Press, 1996.

Landy, Marcia. *British Genres, Cinema and Society, 1930–1960*. Princeton, N.J.: Princeton University Press, 1991.

MacCabe, Colin, and Olivia Stewart, eds. *The BBC and Public Service Broadcasting*. Manchester: Manchester University Press, 1986.

MacGregor, Jeff. "The Naughty Surreal Pleasures of the 'Python' 6." *New York Times*, June 21, 1998, ARTS 35.

Maley, William. "Centralisation and Censorship." In *The BBC and Public Service Broadcasting*, ed. Colin MacCabe and Olivia Stewart, 32–46. Manchester: Manchester University Press, 1986.

Manevich, Lev. *The Language of the New Media*. Boston: MIT Press, 2001.

Margolis, Jonathon. *Cleese Encounters*. New York: St. Martin's Press, 1992.

———. *Michael Palin: A Biography*. London: Orion, 1997.

Marwick, Arthur. *The Explosion of British Society, 1914–1970*. London: Macmillan, 1971.

Miall, Leonard. *Inside the BBC: British Broadcasting Characters*. London: Weidenfeld and Nicolson, 1994.

Miller, Jeffrey S. *Something Completely Different: British Television and American Culture*. Minneapolis: University of Minnesota Press, 2000.

Milligan, Spike. *The Goon Show Scripts*. New York: St, Martin's Press, 1972.

Morgan, David. *Monty Python Speaks*. London: Fourth Estate, 1999.

Morley, Sheridan. "The Complete and Utter Palin and Jones in a Two Man Python Team." *London Times Saturday Review*, March 29, 1975, 9.

Mulrine, Anne. "Off to the Flying Circus: Comedy's New Stars Silly-Walk in the Footsteps of Monty Python." *U.S. News and World Report*, March 23, 1998, 64.

Murphy, Robert. *Sixties British Cinema*. London: BFI.

Neale, Steve, and Frank Krutnik. *Popular Film and Television Comedy*. London: Routledge, 1990.

O'Connor, John J. "Monty Python's Flying Circus—A Soufflé of Lunacy." *New York Times*, November 10, 1974, D33.

Perry, George. *And Now for Something Completely Different: Life of Python*. London: Pavilion, 1983.

Pythons, The. *The Complete Monty Python's Flying Circus: All the Words*. 2 vols. New York: Pantheon, 1989.

Reynolds, Stanley. "Bargain for the BBC." *London Times*, September 16, 1970, 13.

———. "The Rise and Rise of Monty Python." *The Times*, December 14, 1970, 6.

Richards, Jeffrey. *Films and British National Identity*. Manchester: Manchester University Press, 1997.

Said, Edward. *Representations of the Intellectual: The 1993 Reith Lectures*. New York: Vintage, 1994.

Schickel, Richard. "Legendary Lunacy." *Time*, May 26, 1975, 56–59.

Schmidt, William E. "Still Zany, Python and Cult Turn 25." *New York Times*, September 24, 1994, C13, C20.

Smith, Anthony. "Licenses and Liberty: Public Service Broadcasting in Britain." In *The BBC and Public Service Broadcasting*, ed. Colin MacCabe and Olivia Stewart, 1–21. Manchester: Manchester University Press, 1986.

———, ed. *Television: An International History*. Oxford: Oxford University Press, 1998.

Sterritt, David, and Lucille Rhodes. "Monty Python: Lust for Glory." *Cineaste* 26, no. 14 (Fall 2001): 18–23.

Street, Sarah. *British National Cinema*. London: Routledge, 1997.

———. *Transatlantic Crossings: British Feature Films in the USA*. New York: Continuum, 2002.

Thompson, John O. *Monty Python: Complete and Utter Theory of the Grotesque*. London: BFI, 1982.

T. J. F. "Michael Palin." *Current Biography* (February 2000): 59–64.

Unger, Arthur. "Monty Python Invades US Commercial TV." *Christian Science Monitor*, October 2, 1975, 22.

Weber, Bruce. "Something Completely Nostalgic." *New York Times*, March 9, 1998, E1, E6.

Wheatcroft, Geoffrey. "Who Needs the BBC?" *Atlantic Monthly* (March 2001): 2.

Willen, Andrew. "Not Funny." *New Statesman*, October 18, 1996, 49.

Williams, Raymond. *Television: Technology and Cultural Form*. New York: Schocken Books, 1975.

Wilmut, Roger. *From Fringe to Flying Circus*. London: Methuen, 1980.

Zito, Tom. "A Python in the Center of the Ring." *Washington Post*, May 10, 1975, D1, D2.

INDEX